BORDER VIGILS

KEEPING MIGRANTS OUT
OF THE RICH WORLD

JEREMY HARDING

VERSO
London • New York

First published by Verso 2012
© Jeremy Harding 2012

Much of the material in this book appeared in an earlier form in
The Uninvited: Refugees at the Rich Man's Gate (Profile Books 2000)
and in the *London Review of Books*

3 5 7 9 10 8 6 4 2

Verso
UK: 6 Meard Street, London W1F 0EG
US: 20 Jay Street, Suite 1010, Brooklyn, NY 11201
www.versobooks.com

Verso is the imprint of New Left Books

ISBN-13: 978-1-78168-063-6

British Library Cataloguing in Publication Data
A catalogue record for this book is available from the British Library

Library of Congress Cataloging-in-Publication Data
A catalog record for this book is available from the Library of Congress

Typeset in Fournier by MJ Gavan, Truro, Cornwall
Printed in the US by Maple Vail

Contents

Introduction

This book began as a long report at the end of the 1990s, when asylum seekers were entering Western Europe in numbers that had not been seen for sixty years or more. The arrival of hundreds of thousands of people at the frontiers of prosperous democracies followed quickly on the end of the Cold War. Mostly they came from the former Yugoslavia, but there were many from sub-Saharan Africa, Asia and the Middle East. For these unfortunate people on the move the end of history was never in view. They were fleeing penury and persecution and there were many of them. In southern Italy, the Balkans, on the Mediterranean coast of Africa, you knew it when you saw it: this was not the end of anything. The question, under the circumstances, was whether governments would honour their obligation to grant asylum.

There were reasons not to do so. One, it was sometimes said, was that asylum seekers were breaking the law by travelling in clandestinity, in breach of border protocols. A good part of this book, originally called *The Uninvited*, is about the journeys they made and their points of entry into Europe: about the unorthodox, dangerous routes they took into safe countries, relying on smugglers to help them, and the reasons they sometimes used forged documents or destroyed their ID papers. Clearly, if they could have left their homes in safety for a place where they were acceptable, they would have applied for visas, tendered their passports for inspection and boarded a plane like anyone else.

Asylum applications have fallen dramatically since the late 1990s, and in any case refugees are only a small proportion of the world's population who reside outside their countries of origin. While unauthorised migration is no more than a fragment of this larger picture, it has much to tell us about the inequalities at the heart of human movement and the gulf, in terms of wealth and opportunity, between more and less developed parts of the world.

It was already obvious at the time I was reporting on this complicated situation that plenty of migrants who might not qualify as refugees – by the terms of the 1951 Geneva Convention and the 1967 Protocol – were in similar kinds of jeopardy. Drastic poverty was the main threat to these people in search of gainful sanctuary in functioning economies. They weren't generally engineers, IT specialists, healthcare workers or management consultants who could move about respectably. They were a hidden rank and file of unskilled or semi-skilled manpower willing to sell their labour wherever they could. Like legal migrants, they were following the markets, but to do so they had to share the ordeal of asylum seekers – on the same fishing smacks that left Morocco for Spain, in the same trailers rumbling over the highways of Europe. There is no provision for 'economic migrants' in the Geneva Convention. But as matters stand they are not entitled to a proper stake in the global economy, even though they will work for next to nothing to acquire it.

And so what began as a report about asylum seekers soon became a broader look at clandestine migration to wealthy countries, from the beaches of southern Italy in the 1990s to the US/Mexican frontier a decade later, with an eye on the mounting pressure at the margins of reluctant host states and the measures they were taking to secure their borders. In 1999, just as I'd begun this project, two West African teenagers, fifteen and fourteen years old, died in the rear-wheel casing of a Sabena Airbus leaving Conakry in Guinea for Brussels, where their bodies were found on arrival. These were not asylum seekers, but foolhardy chancers, eager to enrol in the new world order – a utopia of energetic enterprise and ideological calm – that was supposed to open up after 1989, but failed to reach Conakry. It was a shocking affair and much was written about it, but no one said of these young men that they lacked 'initiative'.

Twelve years later, on one of the last trips I made, I sat in a court house in Arizona watching dozens of unauthorised Hispanic migrants on summary trial in a fast-track deportation process. They were shackled hand and foot.

These are the images that stay in the mind when the last round of statistics is no longer accurate and the arguments have all been rehearsed: in the startling, incisive manner of political cartoons, they sketch a vivid story of aspiration, failure and ritual humiliation (chains on the feet). But migration is also a highly technical domain, where modelling and specialist conjecture allow us to look more impartially on the larger conflict between the desire for freedom of movement and sovereign decisions about who may come and go, under what terms. I've drawn freely on the scholarly material and tried to say something, too, about the tensions between migrants and hosts: not just the government of the day and the media to which they answer, but states themselves.

There is an enduring asymmetry between the needs and entitlements of the two parties. Migrants need to cross borders but most are only entitled to do so under strict conditions. When hosts decide that they do not need migrants, they feel entitled to bar them. The needs and entitlements of hosts, in other words, are largely consonant, even when immigration control fails to achieve all their desired goals, while the needs and entitlements of migrants are at variance. Globalisation has made the imbalance more apparent. The need to migrate has not diminished but, since the 1990s, hosts have become far warier of immigrant intakes.

The 9/11 attacks, the banking meltdown of 2008 and the economic crisis have all played a part in the growing reticence of receiver countries, but so has a more general feeling that communities, however they define themselves, are within their rights to retrench in the face of globalisation. States and national economies are buffeted by globalisation – we know that – but individuals, local alliances, groups and classes also experience it as disempowering. Like unfettered markets, relaxed migration seems to threaten the identity which communities are struggling to maintain as gale-force trends, originating thousands of miles away, undo their ability to shape their own lives and surroundings. In this context the arrival of migrants is perceived simply as another instance of the world intruding on precarious local space and making it harder to control.

Ed Miliband, Britain's Labour leader, acknowledged the difficulty in an interview in the *Guardian* in the summer of 2012 when he refused to dismiss rising anxieties about migrant intakes from Eastern Europe as mere prejudice. It is entirely possible to have reservations about immigration while believing in fairer payment for products from the global south. These are no more monstrous than the wish for decent wages at home. Miliband is one of many politicians who would like to recast the immigration debate in the light of 'brutish labour markets' – his phrase – and the downward pressure on wages that UK employers have exerted in some sectors by hiring exclusively from a pool of Eastern European workers. Broadly speaking, this is the counter-argument to open-ended deregulation, an idea whose most liberal application would extend freedom of movement to human beings as well as goods and capital. It is at least consistent to urge regulation for all three; or indeed deregulation, as the *Economist* does. It is neither consistent nor fair to regulate the one but not the others.

I've not rehearsed the worthy arguments about gifted immigrants enriching host cultures – it's obvious they do – but I hope this book will remind readers that poorer migrants who may not excel at a sport or have a theory of relativity in their hand luggage are nonetheless responding to urgent needs of their own when they decide to cross a border, even if they have no rights in the eyes of others; that they move because of circumstances which richer economies have conspired to create; and that migration tends to redistribute wealth more efficiently than overseas aid programmes. Similarly asylum seekers – a group of disadvantaged migrants who benefit in theory from the duty of states to offer refuge – are often in flight because of political decisions approved in the UN Security Council. Though there are fewer asylum seekers now than there were when I was reporting from Europe after the Balkan wars, this is no guarantee that numbers will continue to fall. And numerous or not, they deserve a spirited defence.

The first two sections of this book, written in the 1990s, still tell us where we are now, even if they do so through the prism of the recent past. Older statistics have been refreshed where it seemed in order. Journalism dates, yet the harshest aspects of unauthorised migration remain unchanged and some of these original sections read as though they had just been filed. The story begins in Italy, where thousands of migrants were making their way by sea from Albania. There are two new sections, covering the European Union's growing reluctance to countenance immigration from other parts of the world and the battle between Hispanic migrants and right-wing border politicians in the US. They record the growing emphasis on militarisation, detention and deportation on both sides of the Atlantic. The final part of the book returns to the 1990s, and the border fence in Spain's North African enclave of Ceuta, which African migrants journeyed for months to reach and then waited patiently for a chance to cross. Most sub-Saharans who succeeded ended up in mainland Spain, after being held and processed through an improvised camp. Here, as elsewhere, detention was the order of the day, but it was not the systematic instrument of policy that it would shortly become in Europe and North America.

1

After the French, I had to contend with the American police. On landing in Puerto Rico I discovered two things: during the two months which had elapsed since we left Marseille, the immigration laws in the United States had been altered and the documents I had with me ... no longer complied with the new regulations ... After being accused at Fort de France of being a Jewish freemason in the pay of the Americans, I had the somewhat bitter compensation of discovering that from the American point of view I was in all likelihood an emissary of the Vichy government and perhaps even of the Germans.

Claude Lévi-Strauss, *Tristes Tropiques*

In the mid-1970s, about eighty million people – roughly 1.5 per cent of the world's population – were living outside the country of their birth. The figure in 2012 is closer to 215 million, or 3.1 per cent, according to the International Organisation for Migration. One in every thirty-three human beings: this does not seem a lot, but the extent of human movement across borders is hard to monitor – and the figures are a mystery for those of us who have no idea how many people move in and out of our own neighbour-hoods in a single day, or a year, or the course of a decade.

Migration is not a simple affair and migrants themselves are as diverse as people who stay put. The banker from Seattle who signs a five-year contract for a post in Berlin is a migrant; so is the programmer in Paris who moves to Moscow to work for a Russian Internet company; so is the labourer from Indonesia or

Thailand who is subcontracted to a building site in the Gulf; so is the teenage boy from Shanghai indentured to a Chinese crime ring in New York. Refugees, too, are migrants. Often they share their route to safety with others who are not seeking asylum: the smuggling syndicates known as snakeheads, which induct Chinese women into a life of semi-slavery in Europe and the US, also ran dissidents to freedom in the retreat from Tiananmen Square. These things are largely a question of money. Refugees are not necessarily poor, but by the time they have reached safety, the human smuggling organisations on which they depend have eaten up much of their capital. In the course of excruciating journeys, mental and physical resources are also expended – some of them non-renewable.

In the past, the states of Western Europe have shown a generous capacity to take in refugees. The response to forced movement on the Continent itself, from the 1880s to the end of World War Two, might fairly be seen as impressive. So might the absorption of refugees during the Cold War: far fewer, of course, and mostly from South-East Asia, in keeping with the Cold War commitments of the West. But by the mid-1980s, when numbers started to rise again, states in Western Europe were reviewing their duty to provide asylum. The change was connected with the new availability of one part of the world to another – with the expansion of global access, not least as a result of airline price wars. It occurred at a time when France, Germany, Britain and others had made up their minds that the postwar experiment with immigration from the South was over. Refugees have paid a high price for this decision.

They have also paid for the new prestige of the North American social and economic model – unrivalled after 1989, but all the more conspicuous for its subsequent failings. The racially diverse society is a deeply troubling notion in Europe. The shifting and grinding together of peoples – the tectonic population movements that defined the European continent – were already well advanced, and largely settled, by the time the New World became a battleground between the empires of Europe and indigenous Americans. For

Europeans, the multiracial model of the United States, founded on waves of relatively modern migration, including slave migration – the most lucrative case of human trafficking in history – is flawed. The Right in Europe thinks of it as a triumph of capitalism for which multiculturalism has been a high price to pay. The Left thinks of it as a qualified multicultural success which can never redeem the cost of that triumph.

In both views, the milling of cultures and races and the whirlwind of capitalism are indissociable. Everyone pays grudging homage to the American model of cultural diversity, but European governments of all persuasions are dour about its advantages and alert to its dangers: cities eroded by poverty and profit; the cantonisation of social space; urban and rural societies doubly fractured by ethnicity and class; most forms of negotiation dragged along the runnels of identity politics. And if governments incline to the gloomy view, so do many citizens.

Europeans have different ambitions for their social fabric, bound up one way or another with a lingering faith in regulation. Yet those who call for greater control of the global markets and the movement of capital are easily derided, while the wish to restrict free access to wealthier states for people from the South and East is seen as perfectly reasonable. Often the very people who think it a sin to tamper with the self-expression of the markets are the first to call for lower immigration from poorer countries, though in all probability it would take decades of inward migration to bring about the degree of 'cultural difference' that a bad patch of international trading, a brisk downsizing, or a decision by a large corporation to start outsourcing can inject into a social landscape in a year.

It is nothing new for the non-white immigrant, or would-be immigrant, to have to bear the cost of Europe's fears for its own stability, but the EU's wish to keep out asylum seekers is a striking development. Under the International Convention Relating to the Status of Refugees, they are distinguished from other migrants by their ability to demonstrate 'a well-founded fear of being persecuted'. Many who do not qualify for 'Convention status' are protected by other agreements and various forms of temporary asylum, awarded on 'humanitarian grounds'. In practice, however, the distinction between asylum seekers and other kinds of disadvantaged migrant – a distinction designed to shield the refugee from prejudicial factors such as low immigration targets in host states – has been worn away. In Western Europe, refugees have begun to look like beggars at the gate, or even thieves. Since the 1980s, they have lost most lawful means of access to the rich world.

To governments aiming at low levels of immigration from poorer countries, asylum is an exemption that allows too many people past the barriers. Meanwhile, thousands of migrants whose objective is a better standard of living for themselves and those they have left behind are opting for asylum, or plain illegal entry, as a way to outflank restrictive immigration policies. The result is an expensive game of wits being played along the frontiers of the rich world. It is a worldwide contest, in progress anywhere between the state of New Jersey and Taiwan; Queensland and New Mexico. In Europe, the field extends from the Baltic states to the Strait of Gibraltar, from the Aegean to the English Channel. You only have to go to Kent, or the Spanish enclaves in Morocco, or the coast of Puglia in southern Italy to watch the game unfold.

Southern Italy, 1998. We left the harbour in Otranto just after dark, turned north and ran along the coast towards Brindisi. The boat was crewed by members of Italy's Guardia di Finanza. It was fifty foot or so, with two powerful engines which threshed up the water like a harvester, cutting a straight path visible for half a mile behind us through the rolling waters. The moon, too, threw a line of light, brighter, narrower, scuffed at its edges by the winter swell.

In 1997 and 1998, two or three Guardia reconnaissance boats were out in the Otranto Channel at any one time, in all but the worst weathers. For most of the night, they combed the waters for boatloads of illegal immigrants from Albania. At the end of the 1990s, the Channel became a game board on which smugglers of immigrants and tobacco pitted their skills against the Guardia, but it was the immigrants – *i clandestini* – who caused the real dismay in Italy. For most of 1998 they were leaving from the Albanian port of Vlorë; then, with Italian police surveillance on the Albanian coast, the departure points were moved. It takes about an hour for a good *scafista* and his partner to get their passengers across roughly ninety kilometres of water. They are crammed aboard *gommoni*, or inflatable rafts, with two outboard motors. The *gommoni* run a gauntlet of detection and danger. The Guardia's boats are equipped with radar; the *scafisti* have to negotiate patches of rough sea at very high speeds; they must also hope for cloud cover. But business is so profitable and, until recently, demand has been so intense, that a clear night has rarely deterred them.

From the deck of a Guardia boat you can see the game board in all its splendour. The wake of the boat and the moonlight traverse the waters like linear markers, setting the terms of the contest. As the *gommoni* scud across the Channel, they must keep clear of these two lines: the giveaway light of the moon and the roaming, tell-tale wash of the predator. The first two hours of a night patrol are spent in obscure coming and going, the lines of light converging and diverging. As the night draws on and the moon rises, the brighter path begins to fade until there is only a diffuse, milky light covering the water, and the one line, loitering, veering, running straight again, from the back of the boat. It is the record of one crew's efforts to defend Italy's frail territorial integrity, and with it, the integrity of Fortress Europe, bounded by a single external border.

On the Guardia boats, below decks, radar technicians monitor the waters for movement. A regular signal marking every 360-degree scan sounds like the beep of a heartbeat in casualty. In rough weather, the equipment picks up misleading signals. Twice, what might have been a boat turned out to be a piece of flotsam: a large vegetable-oil drum, a reeling assortment of polystyrene packaging. The vessel was well off the Puglia coastline when news came through from the base in Otranto that there were four *gommoni* on the water, within minutes of the Italian beaches.

The lieutenant at the helm took his speed up to about forty-five knots, flipping the boat over the waves. Garbled coordinates, crumbling with static, came through from the base radio. After a surge of movement that brought us within a kilometre of the coast, we slowed up and hung in the swell. The lieutenant produced a pair of infrared binoculars and gazed through them at the mainland. He handed them across, arranging and rearranging me, until I could pick out the shapes of migrants wading through the shallows, the rubber rafts lying off the beach and the *scafisti* refilling the outboard motors as they prepared for the return journey to Vlorë. It was my first sight of illegal immigrants, tiny, pale and alien, stirring like febrile particles under a microscope. I would have seen them, I suppose, in the way we tend to see them, clambering into our world, importunate, active, invasive, always other than ourselves: *clandestini, irregolari, extra-comunitari*. Headlights moved from left to right through the trees behind the beach: cars organised by the smugglers to pick up the migrants; maybe a few police vehicles speeding to the scene.

No one in Italy can agree on how many people are in the country without 'papers'. An amnesty for illegals who could prove they'd arrived before March 1998 provoked an uproar when it became clear that fewer than 40,000 irregular migrants would be eligible by the terms of the deal: there were thought to be between five and ten times that number in the country. It is not known how many people entered on the *gommoni* in the late 1990s. Some in the Guardia will tell you that by the middle of 1998, there were up to forty boats a night; others put it at twenty-five – which is to say, anything between 500 and 1,000 migrants attempting the passage on the coast of Puglia alone. Thousands were coming from Kosovo, Turkish and Iraqi Kurdistan, and places further afield – West Africa, the Horn, the remains of the Soviet Union, Sri Lanka, Pakistan and China. A decade on and the numbers entering Italy remained high. By 2011 they were mostly Libyans and Tunisians crossing from the Maghreb in their tens of thousands. A turmoil of movement has been taking place along the seaboard of southern

Europe, as people make their way up to Sicily or cross the Strait of Gibraltar in fishing boats crammed to the gunwales. It is difficult to know what will put a definitive stop to this movement or how it might be regulated.

In 1998, when Austria held the EU presidency, it suggested in a draft paper on immigration and asylum that the number of migrants to 'the rich, especially Western European, states' exceeds 1.5 million a year. 'The proportion of illegal immigrants in this total,' the paper adds, 'has clearly increased. It must now be assumed that every other migrant in the "first world" is there illegally.' This figure turned out to be a gross overestimate, but one thing is sure: the muddier the conjecture, the better it sticks, and the association with illegality is hard for large numbers of non-nationals or *extra-comunitari* in wealthy EU countries to shed. For asylum seekers this is especially worrying, because so many have had to break the law first in their own country, then in their putative host country, in order to find safety. Often there is no other way.

Paragraph 1, Article 31 of the International Convention Relating to the Status of Refugees recognises that they may be obliged to use illicit means of entry into a safe country – just as they may have to evade customs and immigration checks to get out of their own – and requires that host countries 'shall not impose penalties' on this account. Yet, with the extension of the single European border in the 1990s, asylum seekers who enter a country illegally have come to be seen as a threat to EU, as well as national, security. At the heart of the EU's thinking about refugees lies the imputation of a double criminality: not only do they flout national boundaries, but they consort with criminal smuggling gangs to do so. As signatories to the 1951 Convention, states may not punish asylum seekers for illegal entry, but to associate them persistently with crime is itself an insidious form of penalty. It leads to the presumption that most asylum claims are bogus (if deceit was the means of entry, why should it not be the basis of the whole claim?) and justifies measures designed to deprive them of elementary privileges – some would say, rights.

The huge forced movements of people in Europe during the twentieth century were always a cause of anxiety, and often outright hostility, on the part of states that took in refugees. But the record suggests that even very large numbers of refugees can be accommodated without disruption to host countries. During the 1920s and 1930s, France received hundreds of thousands of White Russians and German Jews; in the 1990s, Germany – already deeply committed after reunification – took in more refugees from the former Yugoslavia than any other EU member. The misgivings of wealthy states about accommodating refugees are a reaction in the first instance to the manner of their arrival, to the initial cost – housing, school places, social security benefits – and to the tensions that arise, as they have in parts of Germany and Britain, between new groups of refugees and resident communities. The uninvited are a costly nuisance when they first show up: a fact which sharpens official dislike of those who smuggle them in.

The crews of the Guardia di Finanza in Otranto have much to say about the *scafisti*. They will grudgingly admit how much they admire their skill; they will talk morosely about the difficulty of catching them and the leniency with which they are treated by the Italian courts. They think of them chiefly as ruthless profiteers who will put people's lives at risk for gain. Since a clash in 1997 between an Italian coastguard boat and a large Albanian vessel, when around eighty or ninety migrants were drowned, the Guardia came under instructions to pursue smugglers only after they had delivered their passengers. The policy is not always observed, but most of the chases in the Channel take place when the *scafisti* are heading for home in empty boats.

A chase is dramatic and largely symbolic – another kind of contest between the cumbersome forces of the state and a more mobile, unencumbered enemy with few allegiances and no jurisdiction to defend. A Guardia boat can manage a top speed of sixty-five miles an hour. Its quarry is capable of slightly faster bursts, the prow riding up at a rampant angle to the water. Under a handheld searchlight beamed from the Guardia boat, you can see the outboards and the hooded drivers, but as you turn in on the *gommone*, it simply pirouettes in a flurry of spray and slides away. I was on a Guardia boat during one of these chases. The captain forced the *gommone* round several times, turning at full power, until it hit our wake, bouncing wildly over the ridge of ferment, baulking at a great ditch of water on the other side and recovering to steer for home. We made another approach, another turn, a fraction earlier than the last; the *gommone* thrashed across the bows at a tremendous pace and tore into the night; we altered course and picked it up again, pursuing, circling, almost engaging. Things went on in this way until we were halfway to Albania. But it was clear from the first confrontation that the Guardia were up against hopeless odds. In this bruising, violent but strangely abstract hunt, manoeuvrability has a clear advantage.

The organised smuggling of people from Albania is abetted in Puglia by the Sacra Corona Unità, one of Italy's major criminal organisations, which also handles tobacco – now a Guardia priority (as it is for British customs) – and a proportion of the marijuana grown in Albania: the *scafisti* act as couriers. Elsewhere, 'facilitators' offer access to the rich world via lorry, train and sea container. Agents in Asia and Africa receive money for getting people into the high-security areas of airports so that they can stow away in the landing gear of aircraft and die. By the end of the 1990s it was thought that the number of young women being smuggled into the EU every year from the former Eastern bloc and trafficked into the sex trade was in the hundreds of thousands. It is not hard to see why the smugglers are vilified by governments, police and the press. They can foil the defences of the United States and Fortress Europe, carrying a criminal virus into the rich world, a sickness which has its origins – we like to suppose – thousands of miles away.

Some of the best information about smugglers comes from the people who have had to use them. In 1998 at the Centro Regina Pacis, a summer colony for children converted into short-term

accommodation for people caught on the beaches, I was introduced to a young Kosovan called Fatmir. He had taught Albanian
in a private school in his village; he was also a Kosovo Liberation
Army supporter: fair game for the Serbians and a likely candidate
for asylum under the terms of the Convention. Earlier that year,
after his village was bombarded and the school burned down,
he had joined an exodus of KLA from the province. They were
heading for Albania. Fatmir took up with a contingent of about
400 fighters, followed by some 1,500 civilians. He walked for
three days across the mountains, but encountered Serbian police
at the border. Three of his party were killed. He now embarked
on a ten-day detour, attempting another route into Albania, but
this failed and he made the five-day journey on foot back across
Kosovo and into Montenegro. There, he and his companions –
four brothers and some cousins – paid 200 Deutschmarks each for
a ride in a kombi down to Lake Shkodër. They paid another 50 DM
each to be ferried across and, a month or more later, having arrived
in Vlorë, a further 1,000 DM or so for passage on a *gommone*.

The agents who took his money for the last leg of the journey
gave Fatmir the impression that he would be going straight up to
Milan and, from there, through Switzerland to Germany on forged
Italian documents. With him on the *gommone* were nine people
from Kosovo. Most of the others were Albanians. The *gommone*
was not detected and the passengers, around thirty of them, waded
ashore in the dark, led by an Albanian agent carrying a bag of marijuana. They followed the agent through the dark into a coppice,
hid until the police had called off a brief helicopter search, and
after a seven-hour walk reached a ruined house in the countryside. The agent collected more money from all of the passengers
and disappeared, instructing them to wait in the house: 'A taxi will
come and take you to Milan.' After two hours, a small truck arrived
and they wedged themselves inside, but they had only gone a few
kilometres when the driver and his mate stopped the vehicle and
threw all the Kosovans out. Fatmir and his companions walked to
Lecce, thinking they might change some money and take a train
north, but they were apprehended at the station and put on a boat

back to Albania. Fatmir was returned because he was eager not to claim asylum: a number of people who could petition successfully would rather try to get through Italy undetected and lodge the claim in a neighbouring state, where they have a better network of expatriate contacts who can assist with lodgings, social services and, eventually, jobs. This kind of common sense on the part of asylum seekers is now disparaged by European governments as 'asylum shopping'.

Fatmir's second venture across the Channel some weeks later was a success. Once ashore, he simply went to a police station and announced that he was from Kosovo. He no longer had a Kosovo ID card: it had been removed by an Albanian official on his return from Italy (and sold, he was convinced, to an Albanian who could now pose as a Kosovan in order to claim asylum). He had spoken to dozens of other arrivals and discovered that it was quite common for agents to treat Kosovans – and Kurds – in the way they had treated him, first time around. The agents, he believed, wanted only to maximise their success rate. For Kurds and Kosovans to remain in Italy, it is normally enough for them to make their way to the police, as Fatmir did on his second run, and state their place of origin – which is why the agents could dump a group from Kosovo by the side of the road, and rob them, without jeopardising their own reputation as effective smugglers or the chances of their clients' remaining in Italy. Albanians, on the other hand, are mostly economic migrants. The EU disapproves of them and, if caught, they are returned as a matter of course by the Italian authorities. For this group, more careful chaperoning by the agents is necessary. The alternative, for an Albanian, is to pose as a Kosovan refugee: Fatmir's Kosovo ID card would have fetched a good deal of money, up in the hundreds of dollars, in Albania.

Human smuggling is one thing, and human trafficking another. The most concise definitions, based on the International Organisation for Migration's guidelines, were offered in 2007 by Caroline Moorhead in the *New York Review of Books*: 'Smuggled people have consented to travel and when they reach their destinations they expect to be free; the trafficked, even if they have initially consented, remain victims of continuing exploitation at the hands of their traffickers.' Freedom of a kind – escape, safety, success or failure in a new life – is the fate of the smuggled migrant. Bonded labour or sex-trade slavery – answering to worldwide demand – is the fate of trafficked people, including minors; even legal work schemes can turn into forms of slavery in the under-regulated world of domestic service. Yet this clearcut distinction between smugglers and traffickers is effectively blurred, because benign behaviour coexists with racketeering in the same smuggling organisations and even in the choices of individual smugglers, whether they are running boats across the Mediterranean or groups of Latinos up through Arizona. Offered a chance to profit from trafficking, a smuggler will often want to take it. This is a free market. Unauthorised migrants run risks of their own, and assess them to the best of their abilities. One year as a sex worker in Toledo, Ohio, or two as an unpaid construction worker on a corporate pyramid in Dubai: many unauthorised migrants have thought this through. The fog of slavery, where governments can shine no light, descends when the contract was supposed to end and didn't.

In Puglia I became suspicious of the idea that smugglers were a modern embodiment of evil. I didn't doubt their business acumen, or their lack of scruple with lives, or their incentive to traffic – a market incentive – but it was reasonable to assume there was another side to the story and in due course I heard it, from a young man called Adem, another resident at Regina Pacis. Adem was from Pristina, the provincial capital of Kosovo. He left in 1998, at the age of twenty-three, after repeated police harassment. He went overland to Albania and bought a place on a *gommone* for 1,750 DM – about £600 – but the weather was too much and the boat turned back halfway to Italy. In Vlorë, the passengers waited for another run. Together with a new intake that brought the total to forty-two, they set off again twelve hours later on a bigger boat. Adem told me in his faltering, Americanised English that the *scafisti* were 'very good guys'. He'd heard about them tipping people overboard at gunpoint and when, on his second run, the Guardia di Finanza approached the boat moments from a beach, he prepared for the worst. Instead, the *scafista* and his mate worked their way about and put off their passengers in the shallows. The Guardia nearly cornered the *gommone* before everyone was off. The *scafisti* flipped it around at full throttle and lit away from the beach, with a man and two young children still on board. Again, Adem expected to see them dump their charges in the waters 100 metres from the beach, but they took the *gommone* into another patch of shallows and helped them over the side. The Guardia boat was in hot pursuit and Adem believed the *scafisti* were taking 'a big risk' when they set the last three passengers down.

There are nonetheless few Schindlers among the modern smugglers of human beings, and the money is good: one *gommone* with thirty passengers safely delivered represented £20,000 in fees in 2000. It has been suggested that twelve years on the business of illegal trafficking, worldwide, is worth more than $30 billion a year – and a significant part of the business involves a second tier of profiteering, as women (43 per cent of all people trafficked) are herded into the global sex industry and domestic service: refugees have always kept strange company. We think of agents, traffickers and facilitators as the worst abusers of asylum seekers. But when they set out to extort from their clients, when they cheat them or dispatch them to their deaths, they are only enacting an entrepreneurial version of the disdain which asylum seekers suffer at the hands of far more powerful enemies – those who terrorise them and those who are determined to keep them at arm's length. Human traffickers are simply vectors of the contempt which exists at the two poles of the asylum seeker's journey; they take their cue from the attitudes of warlords and dictators, on the one hand, and, on the other, of wealthy states whose citizens have come to see generosity as a vice. When smugglers treat their clients properly, however, they interrupt the current of contempt. Above all, they save lives. In the end, the question of good or bad intentions is less important than the fact that the *scafisti* and others like them provide a service for desperate people, to whom most other avenues have been closed.

This is the meaning of the terse exchange that millions of us have watched at least once in the movie *Casablanca*, shortly before the love interest sweeps in, arm-in-arm with the suave paragon of anti-Nazi struggle. It is 1942; Casablanca is full of refugees who have taken passage from Marseille to Oran and come overland in the hope of obtaining a visa to Lisbon. Ugarte (Peter Lorre), a forger and procurer of documents, asks Rick to look after two sets of safe-conduct papers until his clients arrive. 'You despise me, don't you?' he says to Rick. 'You object to the kind of business I do, huh? But think of all those poor refugees who must rot in this place if I didn't help them. But that's not so bad. Through ways of my own, I provide them with exit visas.'

'For a price, Ugarte,' Rick replies. 'For a price.'

In smuggling and trafficking, price is the main consideration, but it is not everything. Smugglers enjoy playing cat and mouse with immigration authorities. In the mid-1990s, the exiled Somali novelist Nuruddin Farah began to investigate the state of his fellow nationals after the fall of Siyad Barre. Many were refugees in Kenya. Others had made it to Europe, North America and the Gulf. Farah spoke to several of the smugglers who had helped them and soon discovered the relish with which the 'battle of wits' was joined. In Italy, he met a '*xambaar* carrier' or smuggler, once a professor of biochemistry, who was now officially a 'resident' in one European country and a 'refugee' in another. 'What matters,' he told Farah, 'is that the doors are closed ... and we, as carriers, are determined to open them.' Another *xambaar* carrier in Milan told him that trafficking was a kind of 'dare' – a challenge taken up in the dismal refugee camps in East Africa, where many Somali carriers have had to subsist in the first stages of exile. Carrying, he said, was largely a way of helping people to snub the rich nations, 'who frustrate their desire to leave a hell-hole of a country like Kenya by placing obstacles in their path all the way from the starting point of their journey down to the cubby-holes which they call home here in Milan'.

The game of wits, the challenge, the whole rigmarole of clandestine entry – these have never been far from the refugee's experience, but it is only since the 1980s, when Europe embarked with new zeal on its project of seclusion, that they have become so all-encompassing. Among the most important changes is the fact that rich countries now require a visa from citizens wishing to travel from places which are likely to generate asylum seekers. Britain, for example, imposed visa requirements for people travelling from Sri Lanka in 1985 (and broke with a cherished Commonwealth tradition in doing so), from Algeria in 1990, from Sierra Leone in 1994 and from Colombia in 1997. It is, of course, very dangerous for someone who is being targeted by a regime, or an insurrectionary group, or a religious movement, to be seen presenting themselves at a foreign embassy day after day in the hope of obtaining a visa. Even if the embassy is not under surveillance, there are likely to be local staff who will report the application. Safer, for those who can afford airline tickets, to think of a destination that does not require an entry visa, buy a ticket that involves a stopover in the country in which they wish to claim asylum, and make the claim in transit. But this option was closed off by means of the Direct Airline Transit Visa, introduced by Britain in 1998 when a group of Kosovans claimed asylum while they were in transit through London. At the end of the 1990s, travellers from over a dozen countries were required to have these visas to take a connecting flight in Britain: the number of countries in 2012 is nearly sixty.

In addition, airlines must pay high fines for carrying anyone whose papers are not in order, as well as the cost of returning them to their point of departure. 'Carriers' liability', as it is known, is an American idea, which can be found in a Bill that went before the Senate immigration committee in 1903 and called for deportations of undesirable immigrants 'at the expense of the steamship or railroad company which brought them'. When carriers' liability reappeared in the 1980s, the US again took the lead, but there were now a number of wealthy countries willing to follow suit. Airline companies had once been a neutral – which is to say, benevolent – force from the asylum seeker's point of view; ground staff might even intervene discreetly in cases where local security in some torrid dictatorship tried to prevent a dissident boarding a plane. This has changed. The risk of incurring high penalties has forced carriers to act as a screening agency on behalf of governments. By January 2000 the British Government had widened the scope of liability: it now applies to the Eurostar rail link and to haulage companies whose vehicles are found to contain stowaways.

None of this would be so serious if the UN's resettlement programmes could bring refugees to safety. But their application is narrow. Strictly speaking, to be eligible for resettlement, a person must already be in a country 'of first asylum' and still be at risk – like many Somalis in Kenya – or unable to integrate in the longer term. This rules out hundreds of thousands of people, not yet recognised as refugees according to the terms of the 1951 Convention. The resettlement programme is also modest. In the late 1970s, the UN High Commissioner for Refugees was resettling nearly a quarter of a million people a year (most of them from Indochina), or roughly one in four of the world's refugees. By 2010, resettlement involved fewer than 75,000 people – around one refugee for every 150 worldwide.

Little by little, the routes asylum seekers once took to safety have been choked off. The formidable growth in underground 'travel agencies' – document forgers, chaperones, drivers, boatmen – is the result. They are the material consequence of Europe's dreary pastoral fantasy, in which the EU resembles an Alpine valley, surrounded by impregnable, snow-capped mountains. For most asylum seekers who wish to reach Europe, being smuggled to sanctuary has become the only option.

At the harbour in Otranto there are two short rows of prefabricated huts and containers for illegals who have been caught, most of them on the beach, a handful inland. They arrive at the huts drenched and chilled to the marrow. They are shivering, terrified, nearly ecstatic – a state induced by the journey and the fact of having survived it. Their eyes are bright, feverish, inquiring, their faces transfigured by a combination of exhaustion, curiosity and surprise. It's as though they'd tumbled slowly and painfully to earth through rain-logged skies and couldn't quite grasp that they'd survived the impact of landing. Jeans, shirts, sweaters are set out to dry between the huts and, after an hour or so, the men begin milling about, while the women sit with their heads bowed and the children sleep.

It is 5 a.m. There are dozens of detainees in the huts. Two Albanians who are sure to be sent back take out their sodden documents: they have wives in Italy and children attending Italian schools; they have work contracts and Italian tax returns, the evidence of their right to reside here. One is a building labourer, the other a mechanic. When the labourer heard that his mother had taken sick in Tirana, his friend accompanied him back. The time came to return to Italy, but they couldn't get the authorisation from the Italian consulate and anyhow, they explained, it is hard to take the legal route to Italy on the ferry that plies the Channel daily. The *scafisti* soften the ticketing companies and harbour authorities with a mixture of threats and incentives, to ensure that very few passengers avail themselves of the ferry and demand for the *gommoni* remains high. But these two men, who are legally entitled to stay in Italy, attempted illegal entry and that is sufficient reason to send them back. (Imagine a diligent servant lodging in the house of the family he works for. He has to leave for a day, on business, but loses his key. He arrives late at night and enters by a window at the back. The family dismisses him.) The strain on their faces is no longer the strain of fatigue. It has cost them over the odds to get to Otranto and now all their outlay is squandered.

By 7 a.m. medics, finger-printers and interpreters are arriving at Otranto harbour. People are examined for injuries. Migrants often sustain fractures wading ashore in the dark. Children can be concussed by the repetitive jolting of the boats at high speed on rough seas. In one of the huts, plywood table tops have been stood on oil-drums and forensic staff are preparing to take fingerprints.

The migrants shuffle down the line with their hands extended. The abrupt introduction of the illegal alien to the grudging host state begins. In this parody of greeting, gloved hands reach out to bare hands, seize them, flatten them down on an ink block, lift them across the table-top and flatten them again onto a square of paper. Four sets of prints are taken from each person, then a photograph. A group of Kurdish men, some in stone-washed denims, others in crumpled checks with turn-ups from their overnight bags, dig their knuckles into a tub of industrial cleansing jelly and climb out of the hut, wringing their blackened hands. A truck arrives with sacks of sandwiches and cases of mineral water. Briefly the sight of food rouses the detainees; dejection and reticence give way to energy and assertion. Men come forward to skirmish on behalf of wives, sisters, children. As disorder threatens, a detachment of *carabinieri* cajoles them into silence.

There are sixty detainees in all. About a third are Albanians, who will be sent back on the ferry. The rest – Kurds and Kosovans – will be bussed up the coast to the Centro Regina Pacis, to be quartered and processed, and eventually released into Italy with a short-stay permit or temporary leave to remain. The figures for last night's game in the Otranto Channel are now through: twelve landings and 201 detentions along the coast of Puglia. But many will have got away. Rain drives down on the prefab huts. Grey seas fret at the harbour walls. As the first contingent of shivering arrivals prepares to board a waiting bus, a dull church bell starts tolling for Mass.

Whether they'll live or die must, at some point on the journey, become a more pressing question for illegal entrants into EU countries than whether they will find a foothold in the rich world. These journeys are dangerous. But to be driven by attrition is to prefer the devil you don't know, or to give him the benefit of the doubt, and for those who buy passage on the *gommoni*, the devil is vaguely familiar in any case. Rumour and precedent keep the *scafisti* in business. This form of passage is relatively low risk. The bigger boats which fill up with passengers along the shores of the eastern Mediterranean and hang in the offing with hundreds of people on board waiting for the moment to abandon them on the Italian coast are another matter. Death from thirst, sickness, hunger or a full-scale disaster is a pressing possibility.

About three hours after the buses loaded with Kurds and Kosovans left for Regina Pacis on that bitter Sunday morning, a 200-tonne vessel under an Albanian flag dropped anchor south of Otranto, off Santa Maria de Leuca. The captain and most of the crew got away in an inflatable raft, consigning their passengers to Italian jurisdiction, and the Guardia di Finanza began shuttling them off the boat in lighters and reconnaissance craft. The captain had been cruising the coasts of Greece and Albania for two weeks, but some of the passengers had probably been at sea for longer, languishing in an even larger boat anchored off the coast of Turkey, before being decanted into this elderly cargo ship.

Hundreds of bystanders waited on the quays in the lashing rain, watching the migrants disembark. There were many exhausted women and children coming off the boat. One Guardia shuttle consisted entirely of Africans. On the gangways, a ravaged young man lifted his face and bared his parched mouth to the downpour. To a barrage of questions he replied that he was from Sierra Leone and that he'd been travelling for three months. He flicked one hand gracefully, dismissively, at about the level of his forehead: 'Up, up.'

He and his friends had come overland from West Africa. I asked where they'd boarded ship, but the police shut the conversation down. That night I drove along the coast through a violent storm to Regina Pacis, to find out more, but the gates were barred by *carabinieri*. After half an hour an official appeared and read out a provisional tally of arrivals: 169 from Turkey, probably Kurds, four from Iraq, three Afghans, seventeen from Sierra Leone, twenty-nine from Guinea-Bissau, one from the Democratic Republic of Congo and another from Senegal.

In the course of twenty-four hours in deep winter, with Italian security already beginning to deploy in Albania and the Italian Government more resolute than it had been throughout the hectic summer of 1998, 400 illegal migrants had entered the country. The figure does not include those who made their way off the beaches of Puglia without being detected. Statistics for the following year showed no let-up: by October 1999, over 20,000 illegal migrants had been apprehended and for every one of those, the Guardia di Finanza estimated, two or three would have slipped through the net.

This is not the first time that Europe has become a place of passage and confusion. In 1937, with one massive displacement of people following another in the heart of the continent and points east, the Royal Institute of International Affairs in London commissioned a comprehensive survey of refugee movements. To superintend the project, it appointed John Hope Simpson, a persuasive and highly energetic man who had worked in India and Palestine, directed the National Flood Relief programme in China (1931–32) and served as vice-president of the Refugee Settlement Commission in Athens. In the summer of 1938, Simpson published a preliminary report of his team's findings. By the time a full text was ready for the presses in October, he was forced to note in his preface that the annexation of Austria had now 'strained the capacity of absorption of neighbouring countries to breaking point', while the annexation of Sudeten areas of Czechoslovakia had created 'yet another most serious problem, the full effects of which are not yet measurable'. A report commissioned at a moment which the Institute might justifiably have thought to be the high-point of the 'refugee problem' was superseded on the eve of publication by a further flurry of stateless people and evacuees clamouring for sanctuary. Yet the findings of Simpson and his colleagues on refugee movements in the preceding years and on reception and settlement in host countries, were so carefully researched and presented that the finished document, which runs to 600 pages, remains a model of what have come to be known as 'refugee studies'. It also has a bearing on the refugee movements we are witnessing now.

Simpson's mainstay in France was H. W. H. Sams, a gifted investigator decorously referred to in the report as 'Mr Sams'.

France, Simpson noted, was 'par excellence the country of refuge in Western Europe' – it was once again the preferred country of asylum in 2010 – and Sams had his work cut out to account for the hundreds of thousands of refugees from Russia, Germany, Armenia, Saarland, Republican Spain and, as time went on, from Fascist Italy. For most of the 1920s, a high demand for labour had worked in favour of refugee 'integration'. Depression did away with that propitious circumstance – it also marked a reversal in France's vigorous pro-immigration policy. By the mid-1930s, however, labour was once again an issue: indeed, with the population little more than half that of its huge, industrialised and militarised neighbour to the east, something of a national security imperative. On the other hand, tailoring the location of immigrants to the precise contours of demand, before and after the Depression, was impossible and would, in any case, have been a delicate matter, even though popular animosity towards them and outright ill-treatment were common enough. Of the large numbers of Russians entering France after the Bolshevik Revolution, a proportion were thoroughly marginalised. Sams reported that in Marseille, those who worked on the docks 'are amongst the dregs of the cosmopolitan population' of the city. In Lyon, which had one of the biggest Russian colonies, 45 per cent of the refugees were unemployed and living in 'great poverty'. Every night, along the banks of the Rhône, about 100 'bridge-dwellers' were sleeping rough.

Conditions of work, even for the many refugees who had it, were often dismal. Lyon, with its high numbers of émigré unemployed, may have been one of Sams's 'black spots' for sickness, but so was Billancourt in Paris, where there had once been 8,000 Russians in the Renault works. Sams gave heart strain and TB as the main causes of illness in the refugee workforce. Problems of labour rivalry also arose. The two conventions of 1933 and 1938 to which France was a signatory urged that 'restrictive laws' governing foreign labour 'shall not be applied in all their severity to refugees'. The French, however, entered a reservation in the margin about foreign labour quotas – the same quotas, Mr

Sams noted drily, which meant that only 15 per cent of the musicians in a well-known balalaika orchestra could be Russian. The quota system was left in place by the Front Populaire, making it hard for new refugees with qualifications to find a position, while political attitudes tended to harden in industry. Sams hints that the refugees in Lyon suffered at the hands of the French Communist Party. 'The Russians,' he reported, were regarded as 'enemies of Soviet Russia' (a very different objection from the one raised by Lyonnais prostitutes sixty years later when the first young women with Kosovo ID papers began competing with them on the quays).

Still, there were jobs and, under the Front Populaire, a growing culture of social provision. 'In general,' Sams reported from Moselle, 'any Russian with the willingness to work and good health can earn a living.' Former German nationals, too, found sanctuary in France, which in the third quarter of 1933 received between 30,000 and 60,000 refugees from Nazism. Many remained for several years, others moved on to Palestine, Latin America, the US and South Africa. The figures began to fall in 1937, but by now 6 per cent of the population were of foreign origin and there were still refugees coming in from Germany, Austria and Spain, including 'wounded or incapacitated German members of the International Brigades'.

It was the crisis in the Austro-Hungarian, Russian and Ottoman Empires, and the fretwork of successor states created after their demise, that gave Simpson and his team such a wealth of human material to consider. Already, between the 1880s and the eve of the Great War, enormous numbers of Jews had been driven west by the ferocity of the pogroms. By the time the Ottoman Empire had been divested, the survivors of the Armenian genocide of 1915–16 were scattered in camps from Sofia to Damascus. In the 1920s, thousands of Kurds followed the Armenians out of Turkey to settle in Syria, the Lebanon and Iraq. By one count, a million and a half Russians were displaced by the Bolshevik Revolution; a third of these were still stateless by World War Two. With the dismantling of Austria-Hungary and the formation of the Baltic states, more Europeans swelled the ranks of *apatrides*, or stateless persons; others found that they were now members of precarious minorities with marginal rights in new political entities, confected by the postwar treaties.

At the end of World War Two, with the retrenchment of the Western empires, mass movement was largely assigned out of Europe: to India, Palestine, Indochina – and thereafter to zones of contention where the superpowers had leaseholder status and a steely readiness to wage war by proxy. During the Cold War, three million people left their homes in Cambodia, Laos and Vietnam, five million left Afghanistan, a million or more were uprooted in Central America, and two to three million Palestinians dug deeper into exile; on the eve of the millennium there were nearly seven million refugees in Africa and many more people displaced inside their own borders.

The end of hostilities between the Soviet Union and the West brought hundreds of aid workers and dozens of refugee monitors – the successors of John Hope Simpson and Mr Sams – back from the tropics to Europe. The dramatic character of events in 1989 and the years that followed gave them a distinctive cast, but in the Baltic countries and elsewhere it was a smeared mirror-image of interwar statelessness that now reappeared, as a series of successor states came into being after the collapse of communism. Punitive rules of citizenship denied 700,000 Russian-speakers national status in Latvia and 500,000 in Estonia. By the end of 1996, UNHCR was alarmed by the 'significant numbers' of Slovaks and Roma rendered stateless, in effect, by the creation of Slovakia and the Czech Republic. In the 1930s, Yugoslavia and Czechoslovakia had been exemplary hosts to large refugee populations. It was now the turn of former Yugoslav and Czechoslovak nationals – Yugoslavs, above all – to spill across new boundaries in search of refuge. Many of the elements that had led to the massive evictions of the interwar years were once again in place, but the idea of sanctuary had withered.

*   *   *

Western Europe was reluctant to intervene until the last minute in Bosnia, but at the end of the 1990s, with very high numbers of refugees already exiled from the former Yugoslavia and thousands more arriving from Kosovo, it was impossible to quarantine the Balkans any longer. The many asylum seekers who breached the fortress, and to whom, in the end, Germany and others opened their doors, were a pressing consideration in the Nato air campaign of 1999. A regime that had confined the effects of its misdeeds within its own borders might have fared better, but Slobodan Milosevic's policies were foisting large numbers of terrified people on prosperous nations that wanted nothing to do with them. That was one of the issues that the European members of Nato had in mind when they spoke of a 'humanitarian crisis'. Tens of thousands of Kosovans had already lodged asylum claims in the EU before Nato began its air strikes. The Albanian *scafisti* ferried hundreds across the Otranto Channel every week, while others struck out overland for Western Europe. The EU looked on with growing dismay.

Yet the extraordinary deportations with which Serbia responded to the Nato intervention made these movements look trifling by comparison. In a matter of months, the number of deportees in Macedonia and Albania stood at around half a million. This was by no means the biggest post-World War Two eviction in Europe: the brutal 'transfer' of ethnic Germans from Eastern Europe after World War Two took five years, involved twelve million people and cost at least 500,000 lives. Yet the Kosovo deportations, trifling by comparison, were shocking to those of us who never knew about the postwar persecution of ethnic Germans. The speed and intensity of the process in Kosovo gave it the appearance of rapid flight from a natural disaster.

There were fewer media organisations on hand to record the earlier movements of people on a similar scale in Europe. To get from Skopje, the Macedonian capital, to the country's border with Kosovo during Nato's bombing campaign, you had to negotiate a double barrier of police and military roadblocks and then, as you approached the gantries of Macedonian customs and immigration, a vast array of foreign journalists. The field at Blace, where perhaps 40,000 refugees were confined by the Macedonian Government, became the focus of round-the-clock scrutiny by hundreds of digital camcorders and telephoto lenses. It was as though the world had dispatched emissaries to record the arrival of an unknown life form, now evolving in a vast crater of mud and bodily waste. The refugees were cordoned off, victims of a three-fold dispossession: forced from their homes and relieved of their belongings by Milosevic; denounced and immobilised by the government of Macedonia; inspected – though hardly addressed – by the media. Stateless, defenceless and finally voiceless. Eventually, posing as emergency workers to slip through the police lines, the press were able to enter the field and talk directly with people who had no idea when or how their ordeal would end.

Gaps began appearing in the screen of objectification thrown up around them, but these did nothing to alleviate the mixture of apprehension and dislike with which the intruders were greeted in Macedonia. Here, above all, they were seen as a potential threat to national stability (and 'Slav' ascendancy), already under pressure from the country's Albanian minority. The desultory tones of Western governments – slow to offer support to the Macedonians in the face of this extraordinary crisis – gave rise to anger. There was much to extenuate the reaction of this little country to the overwhelming influx of refugees – it was no worse than the worst reactions in wealthier countries to the arrival of Kosovans – but in the end, it looked very much like a version of the same hostility that had driven people from their homes in the first place.

In *The Origins of Totalitarianism*, Hannah Arendt remarked that 'those whom the persecutor had singled out as the scum of the earth – Jews, Trotskyites etc – actually were received as scum of the earth everywhere.' She was writing about the 'denationalisations' of the 1930s under Hitler and Stalin. The Kosovan refugees fleeing into Albania were spared the indignities of the field at Blace. They came in carts, towed by tractors, along the flaring snowline of Pastrik, down into a country that existed only in name, but which was once the lodestone of every militant Kosovan's irredentist dreams. Here they were lodged by distant Albanian cousins: in Kukes, in the north of Albania, I saw twenty-six people living in an apartment that a family of four could have managed in Slough or Sarcelles. Yet there was a bitter aftertaste to this draught of hospitality, for it proved that blood and filiation are the best guarantees of sanctuary and that outside their clan, refugees have little to fall back on. In millions of cases, to be an asylum seeker is to be a stranger on trial. He is accused of nothing more palpable than his intentions, but these are assumed to be bad and the burden of proof rests with the defence. The ethnic Albanians forced out of Kosovo into Macedonia were not even put in the dock.

Reviewing what had happened during the 1930s, Arendt wrote at length about the capacity of nation states to project their prejudices. (Of these she had first-hand knowledge: she had left Germany in 1933, after a run-in with the Gestapo, and worked in Paris for a youth organisation, arranging the transfer of Jewish orphans to Palestine.) She believed that it was a simple matter for a totalitarian regime to ensure that the people it had turned into outcasts were received as outcasts wherever they went. She refers to an extract from a circular put out in 1938 by the German ministry of Foreign Affairs to its diplomatic staff abroad: 'The influx of Jews in all parts of the world invokes the opposition of the native population and thereby forms the best propaganda for the German Jewish policy ... The poorer and therefore more burdensome the immigrating Jew is to the country absorbing him, the stronger the reaction of the country.' Arendt was confident that this is more or less what happened. 'Those whom persecution had called undesirable,' she wrote, 'became the *indésirables* of Europe.'

Sweeping, certainly, but her remarks catch the drift of the refugee's central misfortune: to be shuttled along a continuum of abuse, a victim of 'persecuting governments' who can 'impose their values' on other governments – even those who oppose them in fact or on principle. For Kosovans who fled to Albania, clan and language interrupted the continuum. But most of the refugees and displaced people created by the break-up of Yugoslavia, including the Serbs, have run a gauntlet of opprobrium that begins when a regime decides that some of its citizens are guilty of 'subversions of brotherhood and unity', or are simply 'barbarian', and continues when those people are denounced by a local newspaper in a country of asylum a thousand miles away as 'human sewage', which is how the *Dover Express* described the Kosovan and Kurdish refugees holed up on the south coast of England in 1998. The government of a country of asylum may not share the views of its doughty fourth estate, but it is bound to take them into account as it draws up measures, such as those introduced in Britain, to keep asylum seekers at bay.

Depriving refugees of their assets before they flee, in order to ensure a hostile reception in countries that receive them, is harder now than it was between the wars. Army and police can raze their houses, kill their livestock, strip them of their jewellery, steal their cars and cash and destroy their papers – all of this and worse occurred in Kosovo – but they cannot intervene so easily in the network of contacts that persecuted communities build up abroad. Once a pattern of departure is set down, as it has been in Turkish and Iraqi Kurdistan, Sri Lanka, Bosnia and Kosovo, the refugee can follow the thread of survival through the labyrinth with help from friends and relatives outside the country who are ready to put up money for the journey or provide support in the early stages of adaptation.

That pattern of support is as old as migration itself. What is new is the ease with which many persecuted people can move money out of a country before they leave. Once a community under pressure grasps the enormity of its situation, as ethnic Albanians in Kosovo did at the end of the 1980s, it begins to evacuate resources. The crucial transfer is psychological. When hope – the simple idea that circumstances might improve – is no longer possible *in situ*, it becomes fugitive. As it migrates across borders, the able-bodied and the educated go with it: often the middle classes are the most visible dissidents and among the first to leave. Redoubts are established in the wider world; jobs are secured and, in time, others consider leaving. The rhythms are those of straightforward economic migration, with a smaller flow of remittances to the homeland: it is pointless to remit earnings to a place where they can be pillaged. On the contrary, the more who leave, the greater the transfers out, as those who remain convert their wealth into hard currency and place it abroad with the help of others who have left. In due course, the free expression of political views, outlawed at home, becomes possible outside: journals, meetings, fund-raisers, levies, numbered accounts into which donations to the cause can be paid. This was the case of the Eritrean and Palestinian exiles during the 1970s and 1980s and the Kosovan community in Switzerland during the 1990s. It is also one of the reasons people can raise the money to pay for human smugglers.

The poor refugee, unlike the middle-class dissident who makes a bid for safety, is just as disadvantaged as the poor person in a stable social arrangement. In Yugoslavia, greater numbers of Serbs have been hounded from pillar to post than any other ethnic or 'national' group. Indeed, by the end of the 1990s there was no larger group of displaced Europeans. Yet of the 600,000 Serbs who have been uprooted once and, in some cases, several times, only a small proportion have known how to salvage their wealth. They too have been prey to the regime in Belgrade. If Milosevic wanted to strip Kosovo Albanians of their citizenship – for which few had much enthusiasm anyhow – he also used the misfortunes of other Yugoslavs, exiled by the wars in Bosnia and Croatia, to slow down the unravelling of Yugoslavia. Their hardship was as severe as anything faced by the many Yugoslavs who made their way towards the rich world.

The Marinkovic family, for example, were interlopers in Kosovo. They arrived in Pristina in 1995. Their new home lay under the shadow of a pale ochre high-rise: the military police headquarters, a source of comfort to Kosovo's Serbian minority and an object of loathing to Albanians. Marinkovic and his relatives lived together in a large room with five beds in a wooden hut full of other Serbs, like them, from the Krajina (the self-proclaimed Serb entity within Croatia). There were several such barracks, disposed around the police building in an overground warren. They had once contained more than a hundred people but, by 1998, when I met the Marinkovic family, there were no more than forty. A refugee is, by definition, someone who has fled beyond the borders of his own country – someone who knows that the only option is to head for open water. For old Djuro Marinkovic, his daughter Anka and their dependants, the process was different. Yugoslavia simply drained around them. Federal boundaries suddenly became sand spits denoting the frontiers of new sovereign entities. When Djuro Marinkovic and his fellow Serbs from the Krajina fled towards Belgrade in 1995, they were making for the capital of a state whose jurisdiction no longer obtained in their place of origin. In the cold eye of history, they were like any Europeans undone by the vicissitudes of the 1920s and 1930s.

Marinkovic was sixty-two when he was uprooted from his farmstead in the Krajina. When the crisis came, he got his family away without mishap. On their arrival in Belgrade, they registered as refugees and were eventually transferred to Pristina. Other options had been mooted, but in Belgrade they were promised that if they moved to Kosovo, they would be housed by the Republic of Serbia. That seemed to clinch it. Marinkovic, his wife, their daughter and her two children became the willing victims of Milosevic's forlorn attempt to shift the demographic balance in Kosovo in favour of the Serbian minority. By the mid-1990s, several thousand Krajina Serbs had been dumped in the province like so much ethnic ballast.

Marinkovic's life had been a long, fumbling, painful descent into the basement of Europe and, after three years in Kosovo, he was ready to admit that he was in the dark – that everything had gone wrong. He told me that he had been interned in a Croatian camp for Serbs in 1941; that in the same year his father had been murdered by Ustashe guards; that his older brother, a Partisan, had been killed in the course of duty and that his mother had become a drunkard. As a boy of nine or ten, he said, he had worked with the Partisans, setting fires in the fields to guide in Allied planes. This, in turn, put him in mind of how the enemy had laid false fires to mislead the pilots – and the memory of these fires brought him round to the subject of Milosevic, the deceiver; the man that he, Marinkovic, should never have taken at his word. In Kosovo there was nothing. The old man lived in miserable conditions, surrounded by angry ethnic Albanians; he received a pittance as a guardian on a building site; his family depended on a regular international aid package of basic foodstuffs.

In the summer of 1999, after the Serbian withdrawal from Kosovo, I looked for Marinkovic in Pristina. Before the bombings, there were two places, apart from the cramped barracks, where you could find Krajina Serbs. One was a miserable hotel, permanently under guard, the other a stone building up towards the city's mosques. Since Nato's entry under the guise of KFOR, the hotel had changed hands and the stone building had been boarded up. Where the Marinkovic family had lived, the sun beat down on the charred remains of the huts. A large radio mast in the police complex had been targeted during the sorties. It lay lengthways in front of the ruins.

The Marinkovic family had not been long in Kosovo – a little less than four years. Now, in all likelihood, they had been pushed back into Serbia proper, along with hundreds of families driven out under the new dispensation, and scores of Roma. As the Serbs headed north, hundreds more Roma – also targets of ethnic Albanian fury – began heading west, replacing Kosovans on the boats from Albania or making their way by other routes towards France and Britain, to join the tide of 'human sewage' in which Dover, a town of some 35,000 inhabitants hosting around a thousand refugees at the time, imagined it was foundering.

Kosovo was a severe weather event in the prevailing climate of crisis and asylum. As it passed, the issues that were pressing during the 1991 Gulf War and the conflict in Bosnia became visible again. The names of places like Blace in Macedonia and Kukes in Albania have already been replaced by others, while both new and older dispossessions coexist on UNHCR's agenda: in 2012 there were nearly half a million refugees in Dadaab, north-east Kenya, and more than 1.7 million internally displaced persons in the Democratic Republic of Congo. Meanwhile millions of Iraqis fled their country after the Bush/Blair invasion in 2003: the tally by 2007 was two million, but it may now have reached five million. The numbers of Kosovans on the *gommoni* from Albania have already diminished, but by 2011 Puglia and other parts of southern Italy were taking in large numbers of people from the Maghreb.

Governments in 'receiving countries' have to hold to the belief that at some time or other the forced movement of people can be reduced, especially in a world where a new ideology of human rights and 'good governance' has begun to hammer at old bulwarks of impunity such as national sovereignty. But there is nothing to suggest that they will. In the meantime, the same sovereign status that was challenged by military means in the former Yugoslavia can be challenged by law in the wealthy democracies, above all in the EU, where recourse to the European Court of Human Rights may produce outcomes that go against an individual state's preference for minimal intakes of refugees.

2

'You have no idea of the cost of forged documents, Mr Latimer. There used to be three recognised sources of supply: one in Zurich, one in Amsterdam and one in Brussels ... You used to be able to get a false-real Danish passport – that is, a real Danish passport treated chemically to remove the original entries and photograph and then filled in with new ones – for, let me see, about two thousand francs at the present rate of exchange. A real-false – manufactured from start to finish by the agent – would have cost you a little less, say fifteen hundred. Nowadays you would have to pay twice as much. Most of the business is done here in Paris now. It is the refugees, of course.'

Eric Ambler, *The Mask of Demetrios*

The central international instrument designed to protect refugees is the Convention of 1951 (it was extended beyond its original geographical limitation to Europe by a Protocol in 1967). The definition of a refugee is to be found in Chapter 1, Article 1, which states that the Convention shall apply to anyone outside 'the country of his nationality' as a result of a 'well-founded fear of being persecuted for reasons of race, religion, nationality, membership of a particular social group or political opinion and is unable or, owing to such fear, unwilling to avail himself of the protection of that country'. The question is how a contracting party goes about the business of interpretation. The wording of Chapter 1, Article 1 might be taken to mean that only persecution by a state makes an applicant eligible for 'Convention status'. This would rule out persecution by a warlord or a rebel insurgency and so, for example, hundreds of thousands of Angolans who lived in terror of Jonas Savimbi's Unita movement during the 1980s would not have qualified for Convention status, though followers of Unita – largely drawn from one 'ethnicity' (indeed, one 'social group') – who were threatened with retribution by the Angolan Army, might well. Again, an Algerian journalist who feared for her life at the hands of the Groupe Islamique Armé would be less likely to qualify than someone who was known to have voted 'Islamic' in the early 1990s and was at risk of summary justice from state paramilitaries.

These are extreme examples, but the notion that state persecution alone defines a Convention refugee predominated in France and Germany during the last part of the twentieth century. Other countries, such as Canada, the UK and Ireland, have taken the broader view that Convention status should apply to people whom a state is unable to protect – which would mean not only that the potential victim of a Unita atrocity in Angola and an Algerian journalist were eligible, but that a victim of sexual harassment or domestic violence might become a Convention refugee. (Canada has given Convention status to Chinese families as a result of the 'one child only' policy.) And it could well be, according to a signatory's interpretation, that the term 'social group' covers broad minorities such as gays, or women under attack by a particular regime – the Taliban, for instance, before the invasion of Afghanistan and most probably in the future, after the US/Nato withdrawal. In Britain, the Home Office has been forced by the courts to consider women fleeing persecution under customary marriage laws as plausible asylum seekers.

Interpretations of the Convention reflect the political priorities of signatory states. Above all, they give an indication of how a state views immigration in general. A country such as Canada, with a more obvious use for migration than a country like Britain, is likely to take a more generous view of asylum. The real effects of this difference are remarkable. In 1996, Canada decided that 76 per cent of applicants from the Democratic Republic of Congo

(Zaire at the time), 81 per cent from Somalia and 82 per cent from Sri Lanka qualified for Convention status. In the same year in Britain, only 1 per cent of applicants from Zaire, 0.4 per cent from Somalia and 0.2 per cent from Sri Lanka were considered eligible.

In Europe in the 1990s, governments were awarding other kinds of status to those they felt were endangered but did not qualify as Convention refugees. Often these dispensations were underpinned by international instruments such as the UN Convention against Torture – Article 3 in particular, which stipulates that no one should be returned to a state 'where there are substantial grounds for believing that he would be in danger of being subjected to torture' – and the European Convention on Human Rights, Article 3 of which states that 'no one shall be subjected to torture or to inhuman or degrading treatment or punishment.' Since 9/11 the West's widespread use of torture and rendition has turned the clock back: Britain and the US are now countries which inflict or subcontract torture in the name of national security, as France did in Algeria during the 1950s or Syria does in 2012. Nonetheless 'humanitarian grounds' are often judged sufficient for permission to stay in a country; sometimes – as in Austria and Germany during the 1990s – asylum seekers are simply left with no status at all: they have been refused leave to remain, but to send them back would contravene Article 3 of the European Convention.

In Britain, 'exceptional leave to remain' is granted at the discretion of the Home Office. It is an inconsistent, opaque and unreliable award, and because it is discretionary, there is very little argument to be had about it. It is nonetheless a means of extending some sort of sanctuary to refugees who are refused Convention status. Although Britain withheld that status from 99.6 per cent of the Somalis who requested it in 1996, 93 per cent were given exceptional leave to remain. In practice, Convention status has tended to entail the right of permanent residence in host states.

Some people believe the Convention is obsolete in any case. 'The present arrangements,' the conservative columnist Bruce Anderson wrote in the *Spectator* in 1999, 'commit us to obligations which we can never meet, so they ought to be repudiated.' He reckoned an annual quota of fifty asylum seekers to be a manageable intake for Britain – in a year when 71,000 fetched up – provided there were interim measures to deal with cases such as 'the plight of Jews in the 1930s, the Hungarians after the 1956 Uprising and the Ugandan Asians'. These are the arguments of the canny shirker, who knows what work he can afford to turn down: adhere to the bare minimum of the Convention when it suits you, spit on the sidewalk when it doesn't. (In 2010 Anderson advocated the torture of wives and children of suspected terrorists.) Yet his objections to the Convention pinpoint an abiding weakness: it was drawn up as the Cold War got under way, and quickly began to serve the West's purposes in the conduct of that war.

The Communist regimes were quick to bridle at the Convention, and by 1965 the US had amended its Immigration and Nationality Act to grant Convention status to almost anyone coming from a communist country. In the absence of Cold War imperatives, the liberal adherence of Western signatories to the terms of the Convention is, with some exceptions, waning fast. In its place are 'temporary protection', exceptional leave to remain, 'humanitarian' leave, 'de facto refugee' status, 'Duldung' (or 'tolerated status') and other forms of halfway house. There is less international political advantage nowadays in accommodating refugees. Far fewer of the people who wish to claim asylum are anticommunists in any useful sense, even if they come from the remains of the Eastern bloc or China. As for domestic political advantage, there is none. Many asylum seekers, if they could get in, would be black; a proportion coming from the east into Western Europe are Roma. Most electorates in the rich world have set their hearts against that kind of influx.

The growing wish to exclude refugees, involving a curious mixture of 'harmonisation', under the auspices of the EU, and makeshift on the part of member states, has enormous negative implications for the Convention. Matters are much as Stephen Sedley, then a High Court judge, predicted in 1997, when he argued that unless it is seen as a 'living thing, adopted by civilised countries for a humanitarian end, constant in motive but mutable in form, the Convention will eventually become an anachronism'. Perhaps it became an anachronism when the ideological conflict which gave it a straightforward application drew to a close. In the final years of that conflict, the means to reach a country of asylum were, like so much else, deregulated: now the market in clandestine entry is booming, as airlines, immigration services and consular facilities shut down the official channels to sanctuary. But the commitment to provide asylum is harder to shift away from the state. Unable to put it out to tender, governments can only hope to marginalise and degrade it.

Britain has been trying to minimise its duties as a signatory for years. It is highly urbanised, and 'overcrowding' is often invoked to justify its reluctance. Germany is not far behind Britain in terms of population density and Düsseldorf, its fastest growing city in the mid-1990s, expanded more rapidly than anywhere comparable in the UK. With 10 per cent unemployment, Germany posted the highest jobless total in the EU at the end of the decade, yet by 2000 it had far more asylum seekers than Britain. It is possible, then, to sustain some form of open asylum policy, as Germany has – and France did in the early 1930s – in spite of other pressures. On the whole, however, if a country is opposed to immigration, it will want to underplay its asylum obligations.

Britain, which received hundreds of thousands of Jewish refugees from the Russian Pale of Settlement at the end of the nineteenth century, was not always a wilting violet. An account of the change that set in after 1900 would have to begin with the extraordinary cable sent to London in that year by Sir Alfred Milner, the British High Commissioner in South Africa, warning that a boatload of wealthy Jews masquerading as needy fugitives was bound for Britain and that 'no help should be given them on their arrival as anyone asking for it would be an impostor.' Milner's pre-emptive strike against some 350 Jewish refugees from the Anglo-Boer war was a good example of the anti-Semitic chaff that had begun to confound British public opinion on the matter.

The *Cheshire* docked in Southampton amid dark suspicions that troops were being sent to South Africa to fight on behalf of Jewish finance while British Jewry was failing to support Her Majesty's war effort. The *Daily Mail* rallied to Milner's call as the exhausted passengers disembarked at Southampton and 'fought for places' on the train. 'Incredible as it may seem, the moment they were in the carriages THEY BEGAN TO GAMBLE ... and when the Relief Committee passed by they hid their gold and fawned and whined, and, in broken English, asked for money for their train fare.'

There are several contenders for the turning point in Britain's approach to refugees, but the *Cheshire* affair is a strong one. The *Mail* enjoyed a circulation of over a million; the *Jewish Chronicle*, the strongest voice in defence of the *Cheshire* refugees, had rather fewer readers. 'Anti-alienism' had begun to cohere as a vigorous, incendiary call addressed to a large public, with governments responding accordingly, while sympathy for refugees became a muffled but powerful interstitial force, at local and national levels, in the form of voluntary organisations and support committees. How little this has changed can be seen from an anti-asylum story in the *News of the World* in July 2009: 'All you have to do to get everything Britain has to offer is to turn up illegally with some sob story of how your own country is too dangerous or that you're a lesbian who'll be shot if you stay there and Hey Presto, it's like you won the lottery! And, in effect, they HAVE.' The *Jewish Chronicle* has done its best to hold the line on asylum. In the 1990s, when the *Mail* complained about 'the good life on asylum alley' – mostly being enjoyed by Kosovans and Kurds – the *Chronicle* recalled that 'similar sentiments have been expressed about numerous immigrant communities ... over the years – including, of course, Jews.'

During the South African War the mood was stark, as it is now, and the Aliens Act of 1905 confirmed a rampant mistrust of foreigners, which the outbreak of war in Europe only served to reinforce. Further restrictive legislation was passed in 1914; Germans were interned and deported; there were anti-German riots across many towns. Britain remained ready to respond to appeals that squared with the political objectives of the day.

Having guaranteed the neutrality of Belgium in 1914, for example, it reacted to the German invasion by taking in nearly a quarter of a million Belgian evacuees. Anti-alienism lost no impetus with the World War One Armistice; by the end of the 1920s it was possible for a Labour home secretary, John Robert Clynes, to explain to a Jewish delegation alarmed about the precarious status of refugees that the right of asylum was not the right of an individual to obtain it but the right of 'the sovereign state' to confer it. The record of the 1920s and 1930s, which John Hope Simpson drew up in 1938, seemed to prove the point. The intake of 15,000 Russians – most of whom relocated to France or the Balkans – and up to 10,000 refugees from Germany was paltry by comparison with the country's showing in the nineteenth century, or with the generosity of other states at the time. Simpson did not foresee that the British government would ease its entry restrictions in the months leading up to the outbreak of war – or, indeed, that it would take in about 50,000 Jewish refugees – and argued with some passion that Britain 'should show a braver record as a country of sanctuary'. More than seventy years later, with the number of asylum seekers no longer at peak levels, bravery remains in short supply.

The underlying problem, Simpson believed, was 'an excessively cautious ... immigration policy', and in the aftermath of World War Two, that caution only increased. The solidarities of Empire and Commonwealth, developed across racial boundaries in the course of the conflict, turned out to be provisional. The problem was straightforward. The British ministry of Labour had characterised it in 1949 as the difficulty of 'placing ... colonial negroes' at a time when there was a need for migrant workers – a difficulty which, the ministry insisted, lay squarely with white employers and the rise of an informal 'colour bar'. Over the next fifty years, British immigration policy was largely shaped by the racial anxieties of voter majorities who had survived two depressions, an on-again-off-again class war and two 'world' wars. Like the newspapers they read, they were quick to foresee impending disaster (and took an alarmist view of the brief disturbances in 1948 and 1949 involving Arab and African seamen in Liverpool, Deptford and Birmingham). By the early 1950s the British public had warmed to a narrow definition of kith and kin.

Restrictive legislation tends to exacerbate migratory pressure. In the countdown to the Commonwealth Immigrants Act of 1962, the Asian and black population in Britain doubled, amid fears that a door was about to be shut. The Act also encouraged those who were in Britain on a temporary basis to opt for permanent residence. Yet, from 1963 to the end of the 1980s, a minimum of 30,000 blacks and Asians entered Britain every year – and this regular intake, layered over the immigration bulge of the 'beat the ban' generation, set the terms of multiracial Britain, or the 'magpie society', as Cassandras thought of it at the time. The Act of 1962, however, was intended to keep Britain white.

The spectre of the immigrant has not receded in Britain; it has simply taken another form. The asylum seeker is now the luminous apparition at the foot of the bed. Maintaining the moderate influx of immigrants from the south and east at millennium levels – around 60,000 per annum – entails a burgeoning visa requirement (by January 2000, nationals of 108 countries needed visas to enter the UK) and far higher rates of refusal for prospective visitors from poorer countries. In 1997, 0.49 per cent of US citizens requesting settlement in Britain were denied entry; the figure for the Indian subcontinent was 29 per cent. In the same year, while only 0.18 per cent of Australian visitors' applications were refused, the refusal rate for Ghanaian applications was over 30 per cent. As long as migratory pressure meets with a disproportionate response of this order from a receiving country, ambitious or desperate migrants – the two are not always easy to tell apart – will consider other means of entry.

Sometimes it is the only way to pursue a livelihood. Imagine an entrepreneur, based in Kampala, who travels regularly between East Africa, Britain and India in the course of his business. He is a buyer and shipper, bringing goods out of the rich world which would otherwise be unobtainable in the communities to whom he sells on. He is also black, which can complicate matters for anyone stepping off a plane at Heathrow or Gatwick: on his visits to Britain, questions about the duration of his stay and what he plans to do are becoming increasingly fussy; it is taking far longer to clear Immigration. After ten years of coming and going more or less freely, he arrives in Britain and has his passport seized. He is told he can have it back when he leaves. He duly presents himself to Immigration at the end of his stay; he is given his passport, but finds that his visa has been struck through. He is told that he will not be admitted to Britain again. This was precisely the case of a Ugandan trader whose visa was cancelled, he said, for no good reason. Immigration, he concluded, couldn't accept that an honest African might be able to afford a holiday or an airline ticket – asylum seekers were a much easier category to deal with. Accordingly, on his return to Uganda, he arranged for a new passport and, on his next visit to the UK, he claimed asylum. The last thing he wanted was to be classified as a refugee, but he had a business to run and a family to support.

There is no doubt that people who are not eligible for asylum are trying to claim it – and the numbers may well be high. One of the clumsier deceptions has been to pose as the national of a country where there is enough civil and military disruption to increase your chances of asylum. It was not uncommon fifteen years ago for Pakistanis to claim they were Afghans or for Albanians to claim they were Kosovans. One case, the French police in Calais told *Libération* in 1999, involved 'an African trying to make out he was from Kosovo'. Nobody bought that. It happens all over Europe. Moroccans, for example, pretend to be Western Saharans in order to lodge asylum claims in Spain. In the beleaguered world of immigration officials, the presence of 'bogus' or 'abusive' asylum seekers inflames the culture of suspicion, which sooner or later extends to all applicants, plausible or not. As a result, more and more people who might be eligible for asylum are denied it. The rate of successful asylum applications rose towards the end of 1999, but the Home Office still preferred to show high rates of refusal – counting the number of failures to attend for interview, for instance – since these could be used to adduce a growing problem of 'bogusness' and 'abuse'.

Britain is one among many wealthy countries that prefer to keep prejudice and ambiguity intact as a line of first defence against asylum seekers. In 1999 the government recognised a need for a new body of some sort to assess asylum claims, but since the Home Office would rather discourage these in the first place than improve the determination procedure for claimants, it chose instead to create a National Asylum Support Service. The main function of this service, which came into being in January 2000, was to dispense vouchers to asylum seekers, which they could exchange for food and goods in retail outlets that agreed to take them. The government regarded anything but benefit in kind 'as an incentive to economic migration', and so the asylum seeker's weekly cash allowance was limited to £10. Some local authorities had already begun to operate a voucher system after the 1996 Immigration and Asylum Act – you could see the results in supermarket queues, where cashiers, forbidden to give change, urged refugee customers to top up to the full value of the voucher with a handful of wrapped sweets, a six-pack of instant coffee sachets or a cookery magazine (cover story: 'Going Balsamic'). This, rather than people aiming for specific countries of refuge, is what we ought properly to describe as 'asylum shopping'.

The British government claimed that withholding cash benefits brought it into line with other countries which provide 'support in kind', but if that were desirable, why not look to the great normative model of Africa, which contained around half of the world's refugees in 2000, and simply distribute a monthly per capita allocation of oil, salt, sugar and beans? Of course, the countries Britain had in mind – Germany, the Netherlands, Belgium and Denmark – were members of the EU, and the strategy here was parity of penalisation, conceived in the hope that asylum seekers would not prefer one EU member state over another on the grounds of its being a 'soft option'. The voucher system was so discredited, and so humiliating for asylum seekers, that it was scrapped in 2002.

The reasons asylum seekers end up in certain countries and not others are many. They have to do with colonial history, family connections, relays of information and, above all, with the smugglers in whose hands they put their lives. Social security entitlements come low on the list of priorities for the survivor of an 'anti-terrorist' operation in Turkish Kurdistan who leaves his village on horseback, calls on his cousins, raises the cost of a passage to sanctuary, travels by bus and truck to Izmir or Istanbul, buys a place on a boat to Albania and, three months later, still in the hands of a smuggling network, is invited to step out of a lorry on the A3 and make his way to a police station in Guildford.

The Refugee Council in Britain always argued that the money going into the creation of the National Asylum Support Service would have been better spent on clearing Britain's asylum backlog, which leapt from 12,000 undecided cases in 1989 to 72,000 in 1991. By 2011 they numbered around 450,000, including 60,000 individuals lost without trace, according to the Home Affairs Select Committee of the House of Commons. Britain is not the only country with this problem – it has arisen in Canada, Australia, Sweden and the Netherlands. It is normally solved by formal or de facto amnesty, but the longer it takes to clear a backlog, the likelier it is that the system will become discredited. Once a claimant has been hung out to dry for years without a decision on his status, it no longer matters whether he is eventually refused, since the length of his stay will make it hard to deport him without a public outcry or a protracted legal battle. In practice, most of the people whose applications are finally refused after years of deliberation are unlikely ever to leave the country. This is immigration by default.

Even the lawful coming and going of prosperous people between countries puts stress on their points of entry – there were 86 million arrivals in Britain in 1998 – while immigration officials in the rich world can still be stretched to the limit by modest numbers of illegal migrants. The more freely capital and goods move around the rich world, the harder it becomes to inhibit the movement of people, with the hostility of conservative voters to foreign influx growing in proportion as the ability to restrict it dwindles. In the normal way of things – that is, peaceably – the power of government to reverse this process is no greater than it was in the past, but its capacity to signal an intention, and project that signal, is far stronger.

This was not always the case. In 1916 there were riots in Fulham, a part of London plagued by poverty and housing shortages. Fulham was also a reception area for Belgian evacuees. Residents believed the Belgians were receiving higher benefits than families of British servicemen dying in the trenches. The response to the riots was a policy of compulsory conscription for Belgian males. The scrutiny of the liberal press and the Internet, as well as, the influential voice of the voluntary sector would make a similar response nowadays – round-ups and mass deportations of rejected asylum seekers, for example – harder for a government to envisage, especially in peacetime, however popular it might be with certain sections of the electorate.

In 1937, at the height of the Spanish Civil War, the British Government was pressured by anti-fascist groups and charitable organisations into accepting 4,000 Basque children. They were camped out on farmland in the Kent countryside. The news that Bilbao had fallen led to uproar among the children, some of whom left the camp in the hope of returning and enlisting with the Republic. Within days, the settlement had been summarily dispersed and brothers and sisters separated, as they were packed off to remote parts of England and Wales. The Vietnamese refugees who came in under the UN programme in the 1970s and 1980s were also obliged to disperse to locations designated by the British Government. Refugees are at the mercy of governments with stern faces – but so is the anti-immigration voter, who regards cuts in cash handouts to asylum seekers and compulsory dispersal as signs that the party of power has his interests at heart. But that is all they are: signs.

Who exactly are they intended for? In some European countries – France, Austria and Switzerland – the anti-immigration vote is significant. In Britain there are a few suspects on the extreme Right, but beyond this margin, it is hard, for the moment, to identify the amorphous sense of insecurity triggered by the asylum seeker. In 1997, three-quarters of the respondents to a survey by the Institute for Public Policy Research (IPPR) agreed that 'most refugees in Britain are in need of our help and support' and only 12 per cent took the view that 'most people claiming to be refugees are not real refugees.' The minority has a keen eye on the media, and bigotry, for the media, is a more dependable story than tolerance. This falls within the realm of signalling, which goes some way to explaining the tendency to minority appeasement in a period of government by semaphore.

More worrying conclusions about the IPPR study are reached by Tony Kushner, a historian at the University of Southampton, and Katharine Knox, a former Refugee Council officer, in *Refugees in an Age of Genocide*, a superb study of asylum in Britain, compiled largely from local historical sources. As campaigning historians, Kushner and Knox were encouraged by the IPPR survey, but dismayed by the fact that, even though only a small minority were sceptical about asylum claims, roughly 40 per cent of respondents were not prepared to disagree outright with the statement that most claims were fraudulent. They take this to prove that 'a century questioning the legitimacy of refugees has not been without a profound and cumulative impact' (an infectious cynicism, Hannah Arendt would have argued, transmitted to their grudging hosts by the regimes that first reviled them). 'Why is it,' Kushner and Knox go on to ask, 'that British governments past and present continue to pay greater attention to the hostile 12 per cent than the sympathetic 75 per cent?' The next question, perhaps, is why a government of liberal persuasion would not consider the reticent 40 per cent worth winning over – unless, of course, it was not a liberal-minded government at all. The era of liberal-minded government is drawing to a close.

London, winter of 1999. Walking back from my children's primary school, I see a young woman from Kosovo heading towards Camden Town. She walks with the privacy and haste of people in big cities, and in that much, she is no longer who she was. Instinctively I quicken my pace, to greet her, but almost at once I find the way congested by a mob of half-recalled people and images, from camps and beaches in southern Italy and the ruins of villages in western Kosovo. After a moment's hesitation, I give up and turn at the corner for home.

Flora was one of two sisters who had left Pristina at the end of 1998, travelled down into Albania and paid their way on a *gommone* to Italy. I interviewed them at the Regina Pacis reception centre near Puglia a few weeks after they arrived and linked up with them a few months later in London, to plot the unsuccessful football career of a refugee cousin. Even though we spoke at length in Puglia – their English was quite good, and they had set their sights on London, where they had an aunt – it wasn't clear how deep the fear of persecution, or the grounds for that fear, really went with these two women. (Had they stayed another six months in Kosovo, they would have come to know it intimately.)

It struck me, on reflection, that my failure to greet Flora had to do with doubts about her claim to humanitarian status as a route out of the former Yugoslavia. A few weeks after meeting the sisters, I'd been to Kosovo and found their family. The father was a jovial chancer, bluff and hospitable; the mother was quite the opposite – a troubled person, shaken by her daughters' absence. There was another aunt whose husband, a musician and a nationalist, had been in prison. I gave the family news of the two sisters and some photos, which upset them. I was their guest for the best part of an evening, but again, I could never fully establish in what way the sisters had been persecuted.

A day or so later I found myself in a village west of Pristina where the KLA had just ambushed a group of Serbian police. There was fresh blood in the snow and a litter of spent cartridges. The village mosque had been wrecked. Most of the houses had already been abandoned earlier in the year, but one family had stayed, and they had paid the price of the ambush in the KLA's stead. Serbian police had dragged them to the scene of the crime and beaten them. The able-bodied man in the house had been taken away, leaving only a limping, terrified family of the very elderly or very young. There were worse scenes in Kosovo before the Nato intervention, but the memory of that particular farmstead would have crossed my mind as I saw Flora again in North London, and the ghost of a moral judgment must have flickered there in passing, too. It was as though I had a model of the exemplary refugee – as though I could only have been convinced by the sight of the family from that abandoned village rumbling towards Camden Lock in their cart, rather than a glimpse of Flora walking along briskly, at ease in her new guise as a Londoner. Who is to say what constitutes fear of persecution? After all, Flora had wanted to be a nurse, and Serbia had cleansed the public health sector of ethnic Albanian staff years earlier.

Refugees can be importunate during their settling-in period. Fellow expatriates provide much in the way of support, but there are still questions, favours, conversations, which any halfway generous character might properly follow up. A cousin who wants to join a football club and then have a scout come out to take a look at him: this is a good example of unfamiliar needs that can disrupt a wealthy person's love affair with his own stress. Spotting a refugee in my own part of the world whom I'd met as a reporter, I was reluctant to engage. My view of the uninvited was no better than it had been a year earlier, when I'd leaned over the side of an Italian customs speedboat and gazed at the minuscule figures scrabbling onto a beach in the lunar field of the night-vision binoculars.

It was even ambivalent, I am sure, on the issue of school, where I'd just left two young children before catching sight of Flora. Dozens of children from the former Yugoslavia attend the school, along with a scattering of francophone African and Somali pupils, all of them with parents or wards who have exceptional leave to remain or Convention status. A sour parental anxiety stirs from its depths at the thought of language difficulties in the classroom and the diversion of resources to cope with them. Much of the time this anxiety is hidden, in silent contention with the one-world equanimity of the *bien-pensant* parent whose children learn about the death of the rainforests. I have instant access, any time I like, to the mentality of the anti-immigration voter.

The abiding thought is that migrants and refugees are helping themselves to scarce resources, carefully stored up by the small consensual communities once known as nations: welfare, public health, accommodation paid for or provided by local government, premium space in the classroom. Mostly we make these nervous calculations sotto voce, but in our discreet whispering and reckoning there is an audible echo of the ranting public speaker in Auden's poem 'Refugee Blues', composed in 1939, as Hitler's armies occupied Prague: 'If we let them in, they will steal our daily bread.' Yet thousands of asylum seekers rely far more on their own expatriate networks than they do on the resources of the state. Flora and her sister, for instance, were offered a choice on their arrival in Britain. They could remain in London with their aunt, in which case they would not be eligible for housing benefit, or they could move to designated accommodation in the North, where they would. They chose London; they were supported by their aunt and her husband for six months or more – enough time to find work – and then moved into a place of their own.

Where asylum seekers do claim benefits and occupy housing at public expense, there's no question that they are competing with host citizens for resources. The more deprived the area in which they settle, the fiercer the sense of that struggle is likely to be. (And dispersing refugees to the provinces in Britain seems bound to repeat the anguish of isolated Vietnamese families in the 1980s and the troubles twenty years later in Dover, where Kurdish and Kosovan refugees squared off against the local youth.) Why less advantaged indigenous people in deprived areas should resent the arrival of migrants is obvious, even though the record of poor inner London boroughs suggests that friction is rare. Yet sufficiency of means can generate similar feelings, even among those who see unrestrained market forces as the motor of prosperous democracies, but would rather not acknowledge that these forces tend to favour freer movements of human beings.

It is clear, in any case, that the earnings and expenditure of migrants – including refugees – in host economies have exceeded the cost of accommodating them in the first place. This is the story of the United States, but it is also true of lesser economies, labouring under the pressure of change. Some of the most impoverished people to arrive in Britain after World War Two were the Ugandan Asians – refugees in all but name – most of whose wealth had been expropriated by Idi Amin. By the end of the century, they had established themselves as a bastion of British retail, with vantage points in finance, pharmaceuticals, engineering and property.

To judge asylum seekers like other migrants on the basis of their likely contribution to an economy is to impose another qualification on the right of asylum which many refugees, damaged by experiences in their countries of origin, may be unable to meet. They are not helped by bookkeeper arguments about the high motivation and usefulness of the newcomer. They need a more open defence, without proviso, which makes no appeal to the self-interest of host communities. The source of that defence, and increasingly of the funds that might be put at their disposal, is the voluntary sector: parish activists, support groups and registered charities – the network of well-informed, conscientious organisations that developed, in the absence of any public provision, at the turn of the last century.

Religion has a role to play in this. One of the crucial links in the complicated route that Flora and her sister took from Pristina to London was a powerful figure in the Catholic Church. Don Cesare Lodeserto, who ran the Regina Pacis reception centre in Puglia, took care of the sisters and thousands of other clandestines by ensuring passage on through Italy. Without the centre as a first base they might well have been put in police custody or returned to Albania. Don Cesare was an uncompromising figure. He had the absolutist temperament, like Naphta, Thomas Mann's Jewish Jesuit in *The Magic Mountain*. He was flatly opposed to bookkeeper arguments and accepted any refugee or disadvantaged migrant who came his way. He also saw the determination of asylum claims as parsimonious haggling on the part of the rich world; the problem, he argued, lay deeper, in the global divide between rich and poor and the economic dependency to which the North had reduced the South. It was pointless to discriminate between asylum seekers and other migrants. God was the judge of their real identity and, as a well-placed clerk of the court, Don Cesare had no doubt that God took the side of the poor. If there was a measure of disregard for the 1951 Convention in all this, Don Cesare's indifference to 'sovereignty' was greater. It was nothing to him that governments felt threatened by clandestine migration. 'The law should not defend the sovereignty of states,' he hectored his listeners. 'It should enshrine the dignity of man.'

Don Cesare's position was founded on intransigence as much as faith. He rejected almost any realistic policy to cope with rising asylum applications and other forms of migratory pressure that rich countries might envisage in the short term. But he made it possible for thousands of people with a tenuous hold on safety to look for something more durable. In doing so, he set himself against government – he had a weakness for contestation and political gamesmanship – because the interests of government were not those of the people he looked after. 'The only real help that they get,' he said with a perverse satisfaction, 'comes from this reception centre and from organised crime.' This was true. It was the Regina Pacis that helped Flora and her sister obtain a short stay permit, after which they left for Milan. There, they obtained forged Italian passports and made their way through Switzerland and France to Belgium. In due course, they were sent back to France by smugglers, then concealed in a lorry heading for the Channel Tunnel and put out a few hours later near the M25. They went to a service station and called their aunt in London; then they asked the cashier to phone the police.

When I finally caught up with them in London, they were unwilling to discuss their stay in Milan. It was obvious that the assistance they received from organised crime, as Don Cesare put it with such worldly candour, had not come their way without bitter negotiation and sexual harassment. They still thought well of their provider at Regina Pacis, part saint, part operator. Within a few years Don Cesare would be up in the Italian courts on charges of harassment, coercion and violence towards some of the migrants he had sheltered. Nothing in the world of unauthorised migration is quite what it seems.

The rights of EU citizens and those of asylum seekers have become major preoccupations in Europe. The two exist in a state of tension. As a result of the Treaty of Amsterdam, which came into effect in May 1999, asylum, immigration and other 'freedom of movement' issues are now subject both to tighter judicial control and to closer European Parliamentary oversight. In theory, this allows greater scope for redress in cases of human rights violations; it should also bring decisions about asylum procedures out of the backroom into fuller view.

For the moment, however, what Amsterdam has done is to affirm that the EU regards asylum seekers and other migrants as urgent business. Urgent, above all, because the real emphasis of the Treaty is on full freedom of movement for EU citizens, and before this can be brought about, greater co-operation between the police and judiciaries of member states is required, if only because free movement for law-abiding individuals implies free movement for crime. High on the list of criminal activities targeted by the EU is 'human trafficking'.

The outline of the Treaty is hard to distinguish through the drizzle of Eurodetail, but it is possible to make out some important changes. For example, non-EU citizens who are already long-term residents in member states should soon enjoy the same freedom of movement as EU citizens, so that (consistent with the Union's pledge to struggle against 'racism and xenophobia') a migrant from Bamako residing legally in Toulon would in theory be able to move to a job in Innsbruck or Banbury. But on the whole, it looks as though extending the freedom of EU citizens to long-term residents will mean restricting access for many non-EU citizens who are desperate to enter. How much worse matters will get for asylum seekers is difficult to judge, but if the EU toughens its procedures on immigration in general, no one will find it easier to claim asylum in the Union. Whether a concerted campaign, led by Europol, succeeds or not, it will probably drive up prices for the refugees who depend on ordinary smugglers and raise the risks of the journey. It must be obvious, after nearly two decades of Fortress Europe, that a war on smuggling, in the name of a war on trafficking, involves heavy collateral damage to refugees.

EU members, meanwhile, have tried to find a way to 'share the burden' of asylum seekers. The impetus, understandably, comes largely from Germany. In 1992 alone, of roughly 700,000 applications in fourteen European states, nearly half a million were lodged with Germany; other countries such as Sweden and the Netherlands – and Austria, naturally – also favoured a move towards greater dispersal. Nonetheless, the figures have undergone a sharp fall since the early 1990s, from 670,000 applications in EU states in 1992 to 260,000 in 2010. Burden-sharing is still an issue, because the rule – agreed in the Dublin Convention in 1990 and held over in the Dublin Regulation (2003) – that an asylum application must be dealt with in the country of 'first arrival' allocates disproportionately high numbers of asylum seekers to member states such as Greece and Italy, at the EU's external border.

Asylum seekers can find ways around this ruling. At Don Cesare's centre, people who wished to lodge their claim somewhere in Northern Europe were normally granted a twenty- or thirty-day stay in Italy, which would allow them to reach a big city and negotiate the next leg of their journey. Refugees often want to go where an expatriate base is already established but, just as often, they have to take what's on offer. A client may say to a smuggler that he or she just wants to get out of a place; the smuggler will be eager for business, but quick to add that he only does Denmark and Germany. Countries taking high numbers of refugees would like compensation from other member states, and perhaps, in times of crisis, a system of sharing out numbers – regional dispersal, in other words. By 1999, plans were underway for a European refugee fund, available to states with a high intake of asylum seekers; but to amount to anything, it would have required ten or twenty times the annual budget of the pilot fund – and a guarantee that it would not be used to shuffle asylum seekers from one country to another against their will. The fund now exists, and though the budget is generous, the emphasis has fallen less on helping asylum seekers to relocate within the EU than on allocations to areas from which they're likely to have arrived, in order to inhibit 'refugee flows' in the first place. There is nonetheless money available for EU member states – €6,000 per person – who agree to take 'vulnerable' refugees from outside the Union.

The Treaty of Amsterdam proposes a set of 'minimum standards', not only for the way in which refugees are received and what entitlements they have, but for determining who is and who is not a refugee. At the centre of the debate, once again, is the Convention of 1951. On one side are the governments of host countries, who believe it is outdated; on the other are the support committees, refugee lawyers and NGOs, who feel that EU states will take the opportunity of 'updating' it to substitute discretionary policies for the exercise of enlightened discretion in regard to their obligations. This is, in other words, a reopening, and a sharpening, of the old quarrel about right of asylum and whose it is to exercise. The Convention should have settled that, but in practice signatory states can prejudice the right to asylum by the manner in which they decide on the eligibility of those who claim it.

There are several criticisms of the Convention: that it was a Cold War instrument which is no longer appropriate; that it fails to address the linked problem of migration in general, even where it overlaps with asylum issues; that it has nothing to say on internally displaced persons (IDPs), who are effectively refugees within the borders of their own countries; that it is susceptible of contradictory interpretations; and in Europe that many of its provisions have been superseded by human rights law. Then too, the Convention complicates efforts by governments to deal with organised crime and – since 9/11, it's said – international terrorism.

Finally there is no provision in the Convention for people driven across borders by climate change. The numbers involved are as hard to foresee as the variables and step changes in the process itself, but even if the most draconian estimate – 200 million displaced by 2050 – is an exaggeration, and even if the vast majority of environmental migrants relocate to other parts of their own countries, we can predict with confidence that some will be crossing borders as 'climate refugees', with nothing in the Convention to support their case at the frontier.

These arguments are powerful. Even so, the Convention and the 1967 Protocol are the very foundations of our thinking about asylum, and some of their most lucid critics would rather not remove them on the risky hypothesis that the edifice has now been stabilised by other instruments and assumptions. Sixty years on, however, most European signatories want the right to confer or refuse asylum – a right they do not enjoy under the Convention, and which as we've seen can only be exercised at the expense of the refugee.

The member states of the European Union do not care for the views of a radical like Don Cesare, but they recognise the great gulf, of which he spoke, between many refugees' countries of origin and the West. At the European Council's summit meeting in Finland in October 1999, the Presidency observed, in effect, that asylum seekers would not be an issue in Europe if the conditions they were fleeing could be improved. An unremarkable insight. For several years now, EU institutions and advisers have been urging the organisation towards 'a greater coherence of internal and external policies', by which they mean that they would like to address the 'refugee problem' at source and that whoever has an interesting idea about how to do so should come forward. So far, the results have been disappointing. Here is the Presidency's list of 'things that need doing' in countries which generate large numbers of asylum seekers: 'combating poverty, improving living conditions and job opportunities, preventing conflicts and consolidating democratic states and ensuring respect for human rights, in particular rights of minorities, women and children.'

Less venerable bodies might have come up with the same conclusions after five minutes under the shower, but the vagueness of
the language should not obscure the force of the intention: the EU
is clear that it wants to reduce the number of asylum seekers entering its territory, and if it could impose peaceful market democracy
on states that produce refugees, it would. The alternative is to
deploy the equivalent of an army and several flotillas along the
common border, but the evidence so far is that a pristine, orderly
valley, superbly patrolled, which stretches from Limerick to the
forests of Belarus will be hard to achieve.

Europe's desire to reduce the number of regimes that punish
or neglect their populations is fair enough. Until it can do so,
one other option remains open. It is known as 'regionalisation'.
This means trying to ensure that the bulk of the world's refugees, between fourteen and eighteen million in the closing years
of the twentieth century, remain where they are: in Africa, Asia,
the margins of the former Soviet Union and the Middle East. In
1999 a High Level Working Group on Immigration and Asylum,
appointed by the European Council, drew up a set of 'action plans'
for six of the countries generating large refugee and migrant populations. Since the idea is to reduce the flow of people into Europe,
these blueprints contain a range of recommendations on fostering
regional human rights and boosting development. Most are innoc-
uous; some are useful, but none is likely to bring dictatorships to
their knees. In other respects, the documents are both controver-
sial and cynical.

A draft plan for Sri Lanka, for instance, noted that it is 'primarily a country of origin of migrants and, since 1983, of asylum
seekers. The ongoing armed conflict has caused Tamils from the
North and North-Eastern provinces to flee to India and further
afield ... Almost 90 per cent of all migrants from Sri Lanka are
Tamils.' The draft also stated that Tamils were at risk of being
press-ganged into the guerrilla movement and rounded up for
interrogation by the government as suspected fighters. On this
basis, you would expect many petitions for asylum on the part
of Sri Lankans to meet the requirements of the Convention or to

Jeremy Harding

qualify them for 'humanitarian status'. The authors of the draft plan are more intent on finding ways to keep jeopardised Tamils inside the territory: they emphasise the success of local projects in safe areas which 'facilitate the reintegration of returnee populations' and 'strengthen the capacity of host communities to cope with influxes of displaced persons'.

The importance of protecting and providing for terrorised people *in situ*, with food, medicine and other forms of relief, is not in question. The danger is that this will weigh against refugees arriving in Europe. In order to pre-empt the arrival of Tamils, the document went on to suggest that EU countries should 'organise an information campaign' in Sri Lanka 'to warn against the consequences of illegally entering EU member states ... and of using facilitators to gain entry to the EU'. It also advised the EU to pursue 'with the Sri Lankan authorities the possibilities of return programmes' for those who had already entered Europe.

Hovering at the edges of this thinking, without quite taking shape, is the idea that the world, or Europe anyhow, will become a more agreeable place if the global figure of refugees can be reduced by encouraging, or forcing, persecuted people to flee on a local basis only – to a neighbouring state or, indeed, from one part of their country to another. Those who take the latter course are not technically refugees, since they have not crossed their national frontier, but their lives are no better, and often worse, than they would be had they gone into exile. At the end of the 1990s, according to the UN, the world contained around 30 million IDPs – double the number of refugees. The virtue of policies which add to that stock is questionable.

In Sri Lanka, like most other countries in conflict, persecution and poverty are inextricably linked. It stands to reason that some Tamils who have not faced the one will make a bid for the rich world in order to escape the other, quite likely in the guise of asylum seekers. Whether or not the authors foresaw it, the implication of the draft action plan for Sri Lanka is that an automatic screening process to distinguish refugees from economic migrants can be introduced simply by financing support programmes inside

Sri Lanka to the point at which the EU deems there is adequate local protection for endangered people. From this it will follow that, persecuted or poor, or both, any Tamil who sets out for Europe must, by definition, be an economic migrant. When the civil war in Sri Lanka ended in 2009, UNHCR counted roughly 140,000 registered refugees in sixty-five countries and embarked on a voluntary repatriation programme. Britain began forced deportations on charter flights in 2011, and continued in 2012 despite mounting evidence that ethnic Tamils who had not been granted asylum were being detained and tortured on their return. Had they really been economic migrants?

The same approach seems to lurk in the High Level Working Group's draft action plan for Afghanistan – drawn up three years before the invasion of 2001 – which concedes the possibility that some Afghan refugees are driven west by poverty rather than persecution at the hands of the Taliban. 'Since the economic prospects in their countries of first stay are increasingly bleak … they decide to move on, in particular to the EU.' They are, however, rather few in number. During the 1990s roughly 100,000 Afghans sought asylum in Europe – nearly half were rejected. Iran, Pakistan and the Central Asian Republics, in which it was proposed to 'regionalise' or, more accurately, confine Afghan refugees in future, already contained between three and four million. Burden-sharing, then, is a lightweight tussle between developed countries. The real burden must remain where it originated – and with those regions there is little evidence of Europe's willingness to share anything very much. After the Taliban were evicted in 2001, refugee figures began to fall, as hundreds of thousands of Afghans returned home. This is no longer the case. Indeed by 2010 the wars in Afghanistan and Iraq had turned these countries into the world's leading producers of refugees, along with Somalia. Yet regionalisation appeared to have become a de facto success: in the same year, according to UNHCR's *Global Trends*, 'three quarters of the world's refugees were residing in a country neighbouring their own', with Pakistan and Iran accounting for about 2.7 million Afghans.

In the abstract, regionalisation has much to recommend it. Exile communities remain within hailing distance of home; so does the political opposition. The affinity of the host culture with that of the refugee makes settlement less painful. Dissident 'brain drain', or transfer of expertise, from poorer regions to wealthy economies, is kept to a minimum. Yet few of these principles obtain in reality. First, refugees who can only move one door down may remain constantly in 'fear of being persecuted' – the Somali camps in Kenya have borne this out. Second, common culture is often only a result of steely management or fragile truce, its fault lines invisible to the outsider. Algeria and Yugoslavia once had the appearance of stable, consensual communities, but in the 1990s they were no longer places where a refugee from a neighbouring state felt safe; the same is true for many Afghans in Pakistan. Finally, loss of expertise may not be a net loss. Many Afghan women, for example, are Convention refugees in the US, thanks to solidarity and pressure from American women's groups to resettle them. There, if they choose, they can mobilise for change in Afghanistan. In the meantime, far more brutal forms of 'brain drain' are going on in Pakistan. The dead body of a 'regionalised' Afghan refugee on the road out of Attock is no use to anyone.

'Draft action plans' will be superseded by revised plans, and revisions of the revisions, until a glut of negotiated drafts has brought the European Commission to a digestive crisis. The early versions testify to the kind of policy Europeans have had in mind for nearly a quarter of a century. They belong in the great archive of our thinking about asylum – and deserve a wider audience than they will ever get.

One of the most striking suggestions they contain is for new outposts of Europe, in the form of immigration officers stationed in the 'regions': monitors, gleaners of information, inspectors of resettlement applications – the idea, as yet, is vague. It might mean no more than an extraordinary consular service: a similar post was set up by the US in Southampton at the turn of the last century to screen immigrants in transit through England. The oddity is that the new vigilance should fall to Immigration – normally within the ambit of a country's home affairs – rather than a Foreign Office department. This may seem trifling, but it alerts us to the disappearing distinction between inside and outside – and the speed at which nations are ceasing to be what they were.

The idea of projecting national security into the heartland of the intruder is to do not with expansion but with seclusion; not with the will to encounter but the will to privacy, at a time when the privacy of states and unions is a dwindling privilege. A redoubling of frontier control several hundred miles beyond the physical frontier is only conceivable when that frontier is no longer an adequate marker of interior and exterior. This is as true for the EU's common border as it is for the frontiers of its members. The mobility of everything they once contained and everything they once excluded, the coming and going, the constant transfer – all this friction on the cordons of sovereignty is reducing their tension. It is in the areas of slack that the game of cat and mouse between smugglers and migrants, on the one hand, and immigration officials, on the other, is played. The presence of immigration control beyond the border will add to the complexity of things, in a world of overlapping and competing jurisdictions. That is part of the game.

Most citizens, like governments, believe that the outer edges of their states should be reinforced. In the wider context, however, it is not consensus within states that matters, so much as consensus across them. The members of a rich nation, or a federation, may respect its borders, yet if enough people beyond those borders see them only as a barrier to safety or prosperity, then they are no longer a matter of consensus, but of dispute. Disputes over borders are also disputes over the extent of sovereignty; in the past they have involved secessions, or rival states going to war. The new dispute sets the desire of individuals to move freely against the will of states to impede that movement. It is not a war so much as a war game, but it puts rich states on a war footing, as they go about the morose task of entrenching their frontiers – and posting watchmen beyond the gates to shore up their integrity.

The drift of high-level pronouncements from the EU is that refugees will still be treated in accordance with the obligations of host states. But this is hard to take at face value, now that asylum seekers are no longer welcome in Europe without being invited – via modest resettlement programmes, a trickle of visas, and temporary admissions from countries in crisis. If they enter by other routes, they must face the consequences: first, that their primary motive for doing so will be seen as economic and, second, that the fact of illegal entry is likely to prejudice their case. For the growing list of governments that wish to keep them out, the best approach to the Convention Relating to the Status of Refugees can only be to assent with much solemnity while reinforcing all the barriers to entry.

3

Dear Uncle ... God be thanked, I am well. I think of you day and night. I have not come to France to play the beggar or the bandit, but to find work and earn a little money and, God willing, to learn a good trade. There is no work in Dakar. I couldn't spend my time all day, year in and year out, *sitting doing nothing*. When you are young that is not *good* ... I have repaid all the money I borrowed.

Sembène Ousmane, 'The Money Order'

A young, personable man who spoke fair English, Hamraz had been in Dunkirk for about a month when we met. He was a member of the Afghan National Army, from the district of Azra, south-east of Kabul. Early in 2011, going home on leave, he was called to account by local Taliban as a collaborator and told he would have to take part in a car-bomb attack on a nearby hospital if he wanted to redeem himself. He couldn't return to his regiment without putting his family at risk and he couldn't stay in Azra, so he left the country. The bomb attack on the hospital went ahead, reducing it to rubble. More than thirty people were killed. He had been on the road for quite a while; his heart was set on the UK, where his cousin had already arrived. The cousin, he explained, had been one of Vice-President Haji Abdul Qadr's bodyguards at the time of his assassination in 2002, and had gone into exile in Pakistan. Eight years later he started to receive death threats on his mobile phone. He was now in Birmingham, and it made sense for Hamraz to join him if he could steal a ride in a lorry and hop the Channel. The West's exertions on far-off battlefields, shaping a world in its likeness, are among the reasons Europe is the place of choice for thousands of people like Hamraz. In ways we fail to acknowledge, we issue the invitation and map their journeys towards us.

In Calais, a forty-minute drive away, a group of Eritrean asylum seekers talk about the war for independence from Ethiopia. They have a good sense of the history, though the oldest would have been ten when the war ended in 1991. Their destination is the UK, but nobody seems to be making a connection for the Channel crossing. They've got this far by dodging the Eurodac identification system, which means that they avoided fingerprinting in the first EU country they entered (probably Greece or Italy). They think of Britain as an easy-going, deregulated country where they can link up with other Eritreans – there are 40,000 in Britain – and find a way of life.

A thin Ethiopian, spooning up a charity risotto, admits very cautiously to a 'political problem' in Addis Ababa, and goes on to explain that his passion is long-distance running. He competed in Serbia, then went on to run in Greece, where he spent several months and won seven races – 'Google me in Greek alphabet if you know it' – but for reasons he won't share he's burned his bridges at home. His distance is 10k. 'Running,' he says, 'is all about this.' He taps his forehead with his finger. England will do more for his mental attitude than Serbia or Greece, and 2012 is Britain's Olympic year: sports psychologists will be queuing to receive him. All that remains is to slip across the Channel.

Hundreds of thousands attempt to enter Europe without permission every year, or stay on when their visas have expired. Calls to tighten European immigration policy go hand in hand with the project of strengthening its borders, yet it is still a desirable place to be, despite the fact that a majority of Europeans would prefer a deserter from Afghanistan or an athlete from Ethiopia to go away. Some also worry about the migrants who are already here: in the vast majority, their papers are in order, they pay taxes and draw legitimate benefits, but there's a nagging suspicion that they are a net drain on European exchequers. In recession country, that makes it easy to cast them as the enemy within.

European attitudes to immigration have hardened. An early warning sign was the growing impatience, in the 1990s, with the notion of multiculturalism. It was a puzzling argument to follow, because the offending item seemed to take many forms. On the face of it, multiculturalism celebrated the ethnic diversity of a changing world: people had different values and cultural markers, even though they lived together in the same societies. Whether or not these differences were welcome was a test of liberal tolerance and the answer, it turned out, was a qualified yes. Europeans took part in the experiment with enthusiasm, even if minorities were alert to any whiff of condescension and said as much. You had to commit to the new environment and learn to inhabit it. Painful reprimands from minorities, in the workplace, the faculty, the tel-evised debate were the stuff of our re-education as Europeans. By the 1980s, in theory at least, minorities and majorities were on an equal footing. It was the new conversation. It opened a pathway to equal opportunities in the job market and local government. And it felt right, for blacks, Asians, women, gays and any number of straight white men.

But not for everybody. There were those who saw the point of diversity, and even equal rights, but who objected to equality-in-diversity, a fatal combination in their view, with its suggestion that the case for home-grown, European values must now be heard on its relative merits, as one idiom among others. This in turn cast doubt on the long story that held us together, with its passage through the Enlightenment to liberal democracy, Europe's unique discovery, which it aspired to hand down across the generations. Identity too was an issue, if people could move fluently between one and another – 'British' and 'Asian', say – or simply hyphen-ate: it called belonging into question. Who were you really? Along with these misgivings came a feeling that minorities could custom-ise the social contract, opting in and out according to which bits made sense in their micro-cultures and which bits didn't. Ethnicity and religion, opponents of multiculturalism began to argue, were blurring an older, consensual version of citizenship, based on rights and duties.

But there was never a debate about multiculturalism without a looming argument about immigration. It's possible to have reservations about multiculturalism while favouring immigration (or the other way around), but on the whole objections to the first turn out to be objections to the second. And the objection to immigration, as globalisation moves ahead, requires even more strenuous entry restrictions than Europe has in place already. So the question is whether pressure from migrants who overstay their visas or come in undetected will lead to the kind of policies – on border control, detention and deportation – that will turn Europe into a federation of police states. The analogy would be a low-level military conflict going on at a remove from most people's lives, at Europe's frontiers, with captives piling up in holding centres, round-the-clock 'removals' and raids on workplaces. Will Europe after multiculturalism look like Europe at bay? Perhaps it looks that way in any case.

In the 1990s, the quarrel about immigration was focused on asylum seekers, as Germany, Britain, the Netherlands and France were locked in a battle of conscience over their duties as signatory states to the UN Convention Relating to the Status of Refugees. There were 'floods' of asylum seekers; they would require housing, healthcare, education and more. Most countries fell back on the notion of 'bogus' asylum seekers. Governments felt they could spot economic migrants, pure and simple, among the high number of uninvited people clambering onto beaches or piling into refrigerated trailers, but it was a delicate issue. In the years of optimism and deregulation that followed the Cold War, a gale of prosperity was meant to sweep through the world's economies. Yet if anything globalisation showed how great the disparities were between wealthy democracies and the rest: developing countries to the south, the debris of the Soviet bloc, large parts of the Middle East;

places where poverty and joblessness were indeed forms of persecution, or tyrannical mismanagement.

Despite a recent upward trend, the twenty-first century has seen a decline in the number of asylum seekers in Europe: around 260,000 applications in the twenty-seven member states in 2010 compared with 400,000 among the fifteen members in 2001. But the number of migrants in the EU is now greater. Before 2004, roughly 4 per cent of the population of the fifteen member states came from outside the Union. Regularisation programmes in Spain and Italy made 2004 the peak year. Today in the enlarged union the proportion of foreign residents is closer to 7 per cent, an increase of about eighteen million people in six or seven years. But many of these are non-EU citizens living in new EU states: Russians in Baltic countries, for example. Net inward migration was about 1.7 million a year from 2004 to 2008 and is now falling. Misgivings about asylum seekers have abated, partly because the Balkan wars have come to an end, but partly too as a result of invidious strategies by individual governments, aimed precisely at reducing the numbers. At the same time, the debate on immigration has become sharper and its terms more insular: an energetic, can-do discourse assures us, in spite of growing evidence to the contrary, that states really are in a position to modulate the flow of human beings across their borders, to the nearest 10,000, in line with their own priorities.

In France in 2011, 180,000 new migrants were allowed in and, as the minister of immigration boasted last month, nearly 33,000 irregular migrants were expelled. For some, the first figure is an outrage, for others the second; both are minor details in a far bigger story. While more and more people are crossing national borders, the figures for those who migrate within their own countries – large countries such as China, Mexico, Brazil, DR Congo – are anywhere between four and seven times higher. In scale alone, they earn their status as canonical migrations. Arrivals in Western Europe since the 1950s are a minor appendix to the canon, but stir up strong feelings among voters opposed to the steady influx of outsiders, especially when a government promises and then fails to hold down numbers, or vaunts expulsion targets (the French target announced for 2012 was 35,000).

Nine eleven dealt a blow to freedom of movement. Like a front-end collision in a car, it triggered a dramatic security response. Immigration policy was still on the road, but the airbags had been released and remained inflated, making it hard to manoeuvre in traffic or glance at the map. The reflex answer was to apply the brakes, even at the risk of veering away from managed immigration to anti-immigration. Not long after the al-Qaida attacks – and an announcement by the leader of the Danish People's Party that there could be no clash of civilisations because Muslims didn't have one – Denmark brought in a round of laws making it difficult for citizens to marry partners from outside the EU, and impossible if they were under twenty-four. In 2004, a bold proposal in Germany to widen the selective recruitment of migrants was struck down and the 1973 ban on foreign labour was left intact. In France in 2006, new laws on family reunification prolonged the waiting time for a spouse's residency permit from two years to three and required incomers to endorse 'French' values. The following year the minister of the interior, Nicolas Sarkozy, began hunting down schoolchildren whose papers were not in order.

Unease was not just to do with fresh migrant intakes: politicians and the popular press were deeply concerned about the people already inside their countries, and host cultures now felt freer to speak critically about their minorities. That's what Frits Bolkestein, then the leader of the People's Party for Freedom and Democracy in the Netherlands, had in mind when he called for more frankness and 'guts' on the subject of immigrants. His position was a direct challenge to the etiquette of multiculturalism.

Once 9/11 seemed to confirm that the moment for discretion had passed, the same position was taken up with gusto by Geert Wilders, Pym Fortuyn, Theo van Gogh and others. The philosopher Baukje Prins ('The Nerve to Break Taboos') called this turn in the conversation the 'new realism', even if she questioned its basis in reality: its force, she suspected, lay in its appeal to an 'ordinary' Dutch person, steeped in native common sense, whose worries had been ignored for years by left-liberal elites. In the UK too, there were 'new realist' voices, led by Trevor Phillips, chair of the Equality and Human Rights Commission, who feared that the British would look back on half a century of multiculturalism as a slippery road to segregation. France, always averse to identity politics, tended to agree.

Caribbean, Asian, Turkish or North African were no longer the descriptions that mattered in Europe. The defining term was 'Muslim': what Muslims did and thought was suddenly central to the immigration debate. Increasingly, the debate was about protecting European values by trying to bring existing minorities into line. In 2004 France banned the hijab in schools and hospitals (and in 2010 the burqa in public, anywhere). In 2005, in a moment of national delirium, riots in the banlieues were blamed on the mosque. When the country returned to its senses, joblessness and segregation in its larger cities came starkly into view. But a series of Islamist atrocities – in Madrid in 2004, the Netherlands (the murder of Theo van Gogh) in the same year, and London in 2005 – kept Muslims under deep suspicion.

In 2006 a controversy erupted in Spain when Muslims asked for the right to pray in the Mezquita at Córdoba, which had been re-consecrated in the thirteenth century as a site of Christian worship: the idea was not well received and in 2010, after an incident involving a group of Muslims at the site, the Spanish bishops reaffirmed the Christians-only policy. In 2007 a tussle began in Cologne over the building of a new mosque in the district of Ehrenfeld. One of the protests against the mosque was attended by delegates from Belgium's right-wing Vlaams Belang and the Austrian Freedom Party. In 2009 the Swiss voted in a referendum to ban the construction of minarets, and the following year it was Angela Merkel's turn to announce that multiculturalism in Germany had 'utterly failed': different cultures could not co-exist side by side and the onus was now on immigrants to assimilate. 'Muslim identity,' the social scientist Tariq Modood has remarked, 'is the illegitimate child of … multiculturalism', largely because of its stress on religion, which is difficult for nativists and secular multiculturalists alike. In Germany, with the last rites pronounced over the parent, it would be easier to bring the offspring into line.

But as Europe tumbled into recession and insolvency, its concerns about Islam were subsumed within a general anxiety about all new arrivals, whatever their origins or faith. In 2008 the Federation of Poles in Great Britain registered a 20 per cent increase in hate crimes over the previous year, mostly in the English provinces: they attributed the rise to the economic crisis. The same year Italy declared a state of emergency after a round of confrontations between Roma and mobs of Italians; the army was deployed to keep order and filter out Roma (and Romanians) at the borders. After a decade of openness, Spain was involved in a crackdown on irregular migrants while offering a lump sum to legal migrants, mostly Latin American, to go away if they weren't in jobs. In 2010 France embarked on a spectacular eviction programme – Roma again – and David Cameron pledged to bring down annual net migration to the UK from hundreds to 'tens of thousands', a fantastic notion unless Britain left the European Union and refused entry to ever growing numbers of British returnees – 80,000 plus in 2008 – rethinking their options in Dubai or on the Costa Brava. In 2011 the Dutch labour minister, Henk Kamp, announced that unemployed Eastern Europeans should be sent home – he meant unemployed Poles – but was forced to back down.

Islam remained a worry. In Germany the maverick polemicist and banker Thilo Sarrazin set out a long list of accusations against his country's Muslim communities. His book *Deutschland schafft sich ab* was published just ahead of Merkel's funeral speech for *multikulti*. But Sarrazin was also alarmed about welfare dependency and idle intruders, wherever they came from, whatever their human rights, and anxious that the suppressed emotions of long-suffering Germans might boil over in the face of these obtuse visitors. The book sold more than a million copies. It seemed that even the Germans, who had received so many asylum seekers in the 1990s, relished the new Alpine chill in the discussion. In 2011, the principle of free movement between Schengen states came under frantic review after pressure from the Elysée. Too many exiles from Tunisia wished to go north to France via Italy, where they'd scrambled ashore in the first place. Last year, the Danish People's Party pressed the country's government to reinforce the frontiers with Sweden and Germany that no longer existed under the terms of the Schengen agreement.

Perhaps none of this is surprising. It even seems to make sense that the threat of terrorism followed by the reality of a banking meltdown and a recession should have forced Europe to rethink immigration – and welfare budgets – in a landscape of joblessness and debt. But Europe has been wrestling with its doubts about immigration since the 1970s, and the vision of an open, flourishing continent – welcoming refugees, proposing freedom of movement as a momentous objective, even for people beyond its common borders – was already clouding over before the millennium. Now the hopes of continental prosperity have been dampened. Offshore Britain is no longer confident it can become an Atlantic Hong Kong, leveraged on property values and a dynamic financial sector. Across the ocean, the US wishes to play host to itself and nobody else for the first time in more than half a century. Immigrants in these places are still needed, but they are not welcome.

Europe's aversion to migrants casts its project in a cold light: union-maintenance and federation-building, like nation-building, come at a price and make it harder for Europeans to look at the behaviour of nations on other continents with a condescending eye. For example South Africa, plagued by xenophobia in the long aftermath of apartheid, as it struggles to put its house in order. At first, minority rights advocates suspected that 'aggressive nation-building' was the reason citizens of the new South Africa favoured heavy restrictions on foreign nationals, or no foreign nationals at all. In 2008 anti-immigrant riots left dozens dead and hundreds injured – and led to voluntary repatriation for many terrified Malawians, Mozambicans and Zimbabweans. Poverty and rabble-rousing in the townships were blamed. Even so, there was a nagging feeling that citizenship, denied to millions for so long, had been grasped with a fervour that could quickly run to violence against foreigners. Mandela was a stickler for the indivisible nature of citizenship, something he shared with the founders of the republic in France – and with their successors. Apartheid, after all, was the ugly sister of multiculturalism. The rioters in France in 2005 were outsiders, corralled in the banlieues, hungry for inclusion. In South Africa three years later, they were insiders calling for the exclusion of the other.

Electorates in the older EU member states know they're stuck with the immigrants they've got – the legal ones in any case – and governments have turned with a vengeance to the issues of post-immigration. Here, the key word now is 'integration', a rearguard policy to ensure that migrants aren't left to sink their roots in the exotic turf of multiculturalism. Fifteen years ago at the Commission for Racial Equality offices in Bradford, I was told that 'integration' was a bad word, like 'assimilation'. But things have moved on and Europeans are becoming bossy about this. Not only are we sure that fewer migrants should cross our borders – an ideal we shall never achieve without becoming poorer, more decadent and highly militarised – but we're certain that the ones who are already here should be thoroughly patrolled, to make sure they speak our languages and grasp the way we like to do things.

The new arrangements have a few ragged edges. In Britain, for example, we don't believe we should invigilate or educate our most troubling minority, flourishing in the upper echelons of the financial sector, or even drop them a hint that, like multiculturalism, the supra-culturalism of the money markets, and the extraterrestrial salaries of managers and traders, can be very divisive. More modest migrants cotton on to this exemption fast, as they toil away at their integration studies. And there's another curiosity. The path to citizenship, or indefinite leave to remain, is littered with tricky questions. Applicants for settlement in Britain who sit the 'Life in the UK' test – compulsory for most – will have to know how many people in Britain are nineteen or under, whether a quango is 'an arm of the judiciary', or a Methodist a member of the Church of England. But if they pass, they will be well informed about duties, rights and indigenous beliefs. And they will have a reasonable level of English. (Acquiring the language of a host country in Europe carries less of a political charge than the issue of Spanish in US schools.) Learning the ropes is empowering. Language, above all, is both the sign and the means of belonging.

It's not as though migrants dig in, rank and file, against integration. Paul Scheffer, professor of European studies at Tilburg, makes this point in *Immigrant Nations*, a judicious account of what migrants and European hosts still have to sort out about their long and ambivalent encounter. He cites the case of Fouad Laroui, a Moroccan economist and writer, with a good grasp of the Dutch language, who worked hard to pass his Dutch nationality test after several years as a migrant intellectual. Laroui mugged up on the 'genealogy of the House of Orange'; he spent hours in the public library and the corridors of the Amsterdam Historical Museum. He cast a cursory eye over the postwar Dutch novelists. When the day came, he explains, 'the procedure took less than five minutes and there were no questions.' Laroui was unimpressed: this was not a real transaction, merely a formality. Not every immigrant is an assiduous swot with a PhD in economics. Nonetheless Scheffer believes that host countries must be more robust – and ceremonious – as they welcome newcomers into societies that are now 'so diverse that they are left wondering what holds them together'. The ceremony, in other words, is crucial not only for the migrant acceding to a new identity but for the host trying to recover a sense of coherence. Scheffer would like to see more ritual, and more frankness.

Two other terms in the post-immigration lexicon: 'detention' and 'removal'. The figures for detention in the EU as a whole are hard to establish, but at least 100,000 people are being detained at any given moment in the twenty-seven member states in connection with unauthorised immigration. As for deportations, the annual figure is closer to 140,000. As Europe thins the numbers down, deportation and incarceration come into play as policy instruments. There cannot be rules without sanctions: even

Amnesty International and the British Refugee Council agree
that an applicant who fails to win the right to remain should leave.
But this principle is weakened in reality by the fact that hunting
people down and sticking them on charter flights, as states drum
their fingers in the last stages of the appeal process, is prohibitively
expensive: recent calculations by the National Audit Office suggested that removing a family of failed asylum seekers costs at least
£28,000 and so the bill for deporting all unauthorised migrants and
their children could be as high as £8 billion. Time is another factor:
to remove every unauthorised migrant in Britain would probably take between fifteen and thirty years at current deportation
rates. But parliamentary politics, too, erodes the principle, forever
invoked on the hustings and then abandoned, as parties of government that promised to move against unauthorised migrants, or
immigration in general, fail to achieve their targets. At the end
of their term, they return to opposition without having to explain
that they made an impossible commitment in the first place.

Migrants have always been vulnerable to political careers in the
making, but they are also becoming the objects of a new, obsessive
field of inquiry, like birdwatching, based on research and mapping,
by an array of interested parties: interstate bodies, interior min-
istries, lobby groups, border control authorities, private security
companies, think tanks, NGOs and contract demographers. The
vigilance to which indigenous citizens are subjected by homeland
security, corporate marketing and ISPs may be equally intense, but
it is surely less insidious. Europeans now take an invasive interest in newcomers: their itinerary, their abilities and disabilities,
their faith, their criminal tendencies, their likely mendacity and,
of course, their loose-footed relatives (partners, spouses, cousins,
offspring) waiting patiently beyond the border.

In the UK the key point to establish is whether a migrant will
turn out to be a net asset or a net drain. The British pursue this
inquiry with an actuarial passion. Start with irregular migration:
in Britain there are maybe 600,000 to 700,000 visa overstayers,
refused asylum seekers and smuggled individuals from outside the
country. Reframe this as a healthcare cost, as the IPPR has done,

and you emerge with a figure of £123 million per annum spent on tending people who are off the books and unable to contribute, even if they wanted to. Next, imagine the cost of education for children who belong to 'irregular parents', somewhere in 'the tens of thousands'. Assume it takes £4,000 per annum to have a pupil in the UK state system and posit a low figure of 60,000 irregular children, to produce £240 million.

Nonetheless, there is a demand in the UK for irregular migrant labour which, if it weren't met, would result in social costs – absence of care for the elderly, for example – and real falls in turnover for businesses that need low-wage, exploitable labour. Typically, jobs (and sectors) that don't appeal to the British bulldog spirit include care work (23,000 vacancies in 2008), sales and retail assistance, customer service, cleaning and warehouse work, agriculture, construction and food processing. We know that legal migrants are strongly represented in these sectors and can take a safe guess – even without reliable figures – that irregular migrants are plentiful. On the economic benefits of irregular migrant labour minus the unrequited costs in health and education, there is not much convincing arithmetic. But in 2009, in a report commissioned by the mayor of London, researchers at the LSE suggested that an amnesty programme for irregular immigrants would produce £846 million a year in tax and insurance revenues. Britain could think of its illegal, foreign underclass as a support operation fulfilling real needs, as the country struggles with turbulence in its cloud economy. In sectors where labour shortages are long-term and acute, irregular migrants don't seem to be taking jobs from British or authorised migrant workers, but there's a price to pay: visa overstays, which account for most irregular migration, are an abuse of trust; unauthorised entry is a systems breach; migrants may have overwhelming reasons in either case, but both subvert our belief in transparency.

The balance sheet on authorised immigration is also filling up with figures. So what is it we want to know? Well, for instance: surely inward migration puts pressure on the housing sector? Migration

Watch UK, which advocates deep reductions in immigration, finds that it does and projects that 'we will need to build over two hundred houses every day over the next twenty-five years to house the extra population arising from immigration.' The Migration Observatory in Oxford cites research from Miami after the Mariel boatlift from Cuba in 1980, when a sudden rise in the population drove up rents by 8–10 per cent. In Spain, as the foreign-born population increased tenfold to nearly five million between 1998 and 2008, housing prices rose by more than 50 per cent. In Britain over the next twenty years, net migration could produce about 40 per cent of the 250,000 new households that will form each year. But the UK is not dealing with a sudden rise, and the Spanish statistic shows a correlation, not a cause and effect. And we cannot predict migration figures in a time of economic uncertainty. The key indicator in the UK – the ratio of house prices to income – suggests that the housing shortage would worsen even if no newcomers entered the country. In any given year only 7 per cent of new lettings in social housing go to foreign nationals.

What of the public purse? The best way to ascertain whether authorised migrants are worth their fiscal salt is to pit their tax and social security contributions against services received. This has been done in several studies. The findings, on the whole, are that disbursements to migrants are marginally lower than their contributions. The exception is the year 2002–03, when costs of services received were higher than contributions. Even so, in the same year the migrant's deficit was slightly less than that of a person born in the UK.

Then again, a 2009 study by Migrant Watch UK finds that immigrants are a fiscal drain: it contrives this by including services to any child born to a migrant and a non-migrant and splitting the difference between the two groups, where other analyses attribute these costs entirely to non-migrants. MWUK is gloomy about the pressures on the educational system: between 2010 and 2020 immigration looks likely to require an additional one million school places at a cost of more than £100 billion. On health services in England, it notes 605,000 patients from overseas registering with

GPs in 2007–08: a figure higher by 100,000 than at least one international estimate of the inflow to the UK, which the think tank takes to mean that large numbers of unauthorised migrants are on the books at health centres.

Migrant studies is not a field for simple-minded Gradgrinds: the data are never quite stable and methods and measures used in the field tend to reinforce the suspicions of the particular research team. Migration Watch is a good example of a team with a mission to curtail net migration. IPPR's migration experts and the Migration Observatory in Oxford admit that some of the findings they present are little more than pointers. The advantage, in their eyes, of discussing immigration purely as a resource issue is that attitudes struck by politicians and the press, quite often negative, can be answered quite simply with the facts, as part of a common-sense debate about how societies create or squander wealth.

But there are disadvantages too. One is that strong feelings aren't always susceptible to sound economic arguments. The demography of European states suggests that they need skilled and unskilled migrants, and that every successful attempt to curtail migration comes at a price that someone else – citizens reaching retirement in 2050, say – will eventually have to pay. The European Commission, the OECD and the two great champions of liberal market capitalism, the *Economist* and the *Financial Times*, are in favour of freer borders and fewer curbs on immigration. The OECD applauds the fact that since 2008, the drop in immigration to member-states has not been as sharp as it feared. Opponents of liberal immigration policy do not buy into this upbeat perspective on globalisation, and their objections cannot be changed by an appeal to good sense.

Another disadvantage is that in an earnings/expenditure analysis of immigration, migrants remain a matter of objective interest only; they cannot really have a point of view. This takes us back with a jolt to Frantz Fanon's remarks in *Black Skin, White Masks* about his sense of his own conspicuousness as a member of a racial minority, and his longing for invisibility. But contemporary migrants, for the purposes of any discussion about motives, are already both conspicuous and invisible: such is the paradoxical attitude of their host communities. Whatever migrants might have had to say, if they can be shown to produce immediate social, fiscal and market benefits, it is all right to defend them against their detractors; if they can't, it is not. If they have needs, they are obscure, and their subjectivity is only grudgingly acknowledged when we transpose it to the domain of rights, charters and conventions, for the courts to deliberate.

In *Debating the Ethics of Immigration*, two philosophers, Christopher Heath Wellman and Phillip Cole, ask whether anyone should be able, in principle, to prevent another person from crossing a border. To have this discussion at all is to restore a degree of intention to migrants, as both writers do, even though they disagree about the answer. For Wellman, freedom to associate also implies freedom not to associate, and legitimate states should be free to exercise both. He accepts the need for a global redistribution of wealth and opportunity – as we'll see, migrants remit vast sums of money to their countries of origin – but argues that 'whatever duties of distributive justice wealthy states have to those abroad, they need not be paid in the currency of open borders.' Cole, on the contrary, wants to sketch 'an egalitarian theory of global justice' and sees borders as an obstacle to fairness: freedom of movement is undoubtedly a right, like the right to freedom of speech, or religious and sexual preference. But only a framework of global governance can found it, manage it and try to ensure that it's respected. Borders, in other words, have to wither away.

The frontier, for the purposes of this debate, is the place of negotiation between insiders and outsiders. The terms are set by the insiders and approved internationally. But it is also a divide between 'communitarian' and 'cosmopolitan' models of rights and obligations. The former proposes a bounded, particular set of priorities and interests, modest at best, narrow-minded at worst: the echoes here are from the political theorist David Miller. The latter envisages a kind of global ethics, ambitious and unwieldy: the echoes here are from Michael Dummett and Onora O'Neill and might be dismissed as utopian, were it not for the fact that human movement across borders is set to continue, with or without an international consensus about how it's regulated.

In Europe, the most startling communitarian defence of the border is Régis Debray's *Eloge des frontières* (2010), a grumpy, spirited attack on the liberal vogue for anything 'sans frontières'. In France the list is long. It includes doctors, pharmacy staff, architects, librarians, lawyers, journalists and firemen. For Debray firemen without borders is an absurdity. The frontier, he argues, constitutes an indispensable limit, like the outer limit of the body. The deepest thing about mankind, Valéry said, is its skin. In this sense, globalisation is a kind of flaying, driving us to a frenzy of one-world generalities that have no grounding in the circumscribed realm of nations and peoples, whose members have to cross a threshold each time they transact with their counterparts. Debray's is not a crude organic description of the nation, more a plea for the specific and the sacred: a plea made by an erstwhile internationalist who doubts the cosmopolitan case. The book is based on a lecture he delivered in Tokyo in 2010, a few months before France began the most flamboyant of its regular campaigns against Eastern European Roma. More than 8,000 were deported in that year. Every disappointed global citizen received €300 for the privilege of being hustled onto a plane. The Roma, who were never multicultural, will continue to be puzzled by the rituals Debray wants them to observe, but the Front National gets the point.

The difficulty with integration remains that for every existing immigrant who might learn the 'Marseillaise' or plough through the history of Dutch fiction, there are a dozen more trying to access the EU. Integration, in the view of sceptics and diehards, is a losers' game unless the pass is cut off and the communitarian model is allowed to flourish. Which is to say that secure borders and symbolic expulsions are essential to underpin the policy of integration. Yet rationed access expresses a deep contradiction in European values, as set out in a range of declarations that pertain to citizens of member states, and human beings in general. We are universal or we are not. On the one hand, gated communities are anathema to the egalitarian ideal. On the other, gating and exclusion are the preconditions of a new civilising mission Europe now feels obliged to carry out at home, as it reconciles itself to earlier intakes of newcomers.

Border abolitionists like to quote George Kennan's realpolitik memo to George Marshall, the US secretary of state, in 1948, with its call for America 'to dispense with all sentimentality and daydreaming' about the fact that it had some 6 per cent of the world's population and 50 per cent of its wealth. Kennan is the countermodel for the sans-frontières. 'Our real task in the coming period,' he wrote, 'is to maintain this position of disparity without positive detriment to our national security.' And later in the memo, as he reviewed the fate of subject peoples in distant countries: 'We should cease to talk about vague and unreal objectives such as human rights, the raising of living standards and democratisation.' The same hard-headedness, as migrant rights groups are quick to point out, now obtains with regard to Europe's frontiers. Ambition, education and wealth send tens of thousands of people from the global south to the global north, yet poverty and disparity are the real drivers, and disparity is more marked than it was when Kennan was at the State Department.

A well-known study of 2006 from the UN University's World Institute for Development Economics Research found that the richest 2 per cent of the world's adults owned half its wealth. The figure gives a good sense of how acute the situation is for the havenots in a world where resources are stretched. The basic needs of most migrants are access to work and sufficient healthcare to ensure that they can earn and remit money to families at home who might otherwise go hungry. Europe is resource-rich by these standards. Whatever happens to the single currency, the EU still contains five of the world's most powerful economies; it remains the world's wealthiest continental bloc, with GDP per capita of roughly €28,000. When you run the figures through purchasing power parity, a relative measure of living costs in different countries, GDP (PPP) per capita in Germany is about three times higher than in Turkey, thirteen times higher than in Pakistan and a hundred times higher than in the Democratic Republic of Congo. The Mediterranean peoples of Europe moved north in the twentieth century to confront this disparity, and the Portuguese – still France's largest foreign population in 2006 – went through epic hardships on their way. The pain barrier is higher now, but others will continue to cross it, with or without an invitation. Europe is still somewhere to be.

Failure and solitude are common experiences for migrants settling in, and among unauthorised migrants, there are many casualties by the side of the road to prosperity. There is humiliation, illness and death. Migrants die in trucks, they drown, they are murdered in smuggling operations or ruthlessly exploited because their business is illegal and the police, in the many countries through which they have to travel, are the last people they would contact. These are the dangers that EU border security points up in its publicity campaigns against clandestine entry. They cast immigration control in heroic roles, saving lives in rough seas off the Canaries or in a first-aid tent in Puglia. And what sinner wouldn't want to be pulled from the pit by a competent saviour? But clandestine migrants scarcely need reminding that there would be no need for rescue without a fatal prohibition in the first place. Besides, the image of humanitarian refoulement has been compromised by the harsh treatment of deportees on aeroplanes and a growing suspicion that migrants in extreme danger may, on occasion, be ignored; in March 2011 around sixty people, embarked in Libya, were left to die of thirst and hunger even after their disabled boat had been spotted from a helicopter and several ships, including an aircraft carrier.

As Europe recoils from the idea of inward migration, its border policy becomes more probing and adventurous. The motto: expand the better to contract. The EU's boundaries are constantly being pushed beyond the physical extent of the union into forward positions from which member states hope to defend themselves against further intrusion. This process began in 1999, at the Tampere summit, when it was agreed that the EU should co-operate with countries from which large numbers of migrants were entering, or trying to, in order to manage 'migration flows'. At that stage it was really no more than an idea, but it was fleshed out at a meeting in Laeken three months after 9/11, where the European Council resolved that readmission agreements should be drawn up between the EU and sender countries. The watershed was reached a few years later, as Frontex – the European Agency for the Management of External Borders – embarked on its first missions outside the EU. (Frontex gathers intelligence about border pressures and shares it with member states; it also puts rapid deployment teams and advisers at their disposal.)

The meaning of 'co-operation' as it emerged in Tampere is to restrict third-country migration to a trickle, and set up holding camps outside the EU where unauthorised migrants can be detained and eventually returned to their place of origin. The most spectacular example was Gaddafi's Libya, where bilateral arrangements with Italy and, later, a generous commitment from the EU, turned the country into a vast immigration and customs outpost with detention facilities for asylum seekers, and funds for charter flights to send 'illegals' back to sub-Saharan Africa (5,000 or 6,000 between mid-2003 and the end of 2004). In 2009 Human Rights Watch reported that the EU was offering €20 million to Gaddafi for new accommodation centres and €60 million for 'migration management' along his country's southern borders. Apparently he was reluctant to sign up for anything less than a €300 million package, but in October 2010 he settled for €60 million and put his name to a 'migration co-operation agenda'.

Libya is not the only example of a forward border post with a mission to intercept and detain (a mission that looks set to continue under the new leadership in Tripoli, which signed a memorandum of understanding with Italy in 2012). In 2006 a school in Nouadhibou, a seaboard city in Mauritania, became a detention centre for clandestine migrants. Seven months later Frontex deployed boats in the waters off the coast. The intention was to cut off migrants from Senegal, Cape Verde and Mauritania at the earliest possible stage in their journey. Spain had asked Frontex for help, but the agency could patrol in African waters only after the Spanish had concluded bilateral agreements with Mauritania and Senegal, as the Italians had done with Libya. The terms of these agreements are confidential and we can only guess what promises Spain made. In due course, however, the EU itself committed money, as it did in Libya: €8 million to Mauritania, for instance, in the tenth European Development Fund (2008–13), for border security and migration management.

Conditions for intercepted migrants in 2010 were harsh. The centre in Nouadhibou had cell-like rooms with up to thirty bunk beds, inadequate light and ventilation and minimal healthcare. 'Over there,' an expelled Malian recalled, 'Mauritanian police officers beat people to death.' But the statistical success of the project was astonishing. Around 31,000 clandestine migrants arriving by boat were detained in the Canaries in 2006. By 2009, thanks to the coastal deployment by Frontex and regionalised co-operation, that figure had dropped below 2,500. An interesting footnote about corruption: in roughly the same period, figures for people going through the detention centre remained stable, at about 300 a month. The likeliest answer to this puzzle is that the Mauritanian authorities are massaging the numbers in order to stay in the way of European aid. A Malian chef in Nouadhibou was arrested and released twice, even though he was a legal migrant, increasing that month's detention figures in the converted school by two.

As European immigration control forges south, it raises tensions between states in Africa. Mauritania's new, indentured relationship with the EU is a source of friction with its neighbours Mali and Senegal. Neither likes to take non-nationals, shoved out of Mauritania, who are supposed to make their way back to Niger, Ghana, Nigeria. The result, according to a 2010 report by Migreurop, is that 'the Mauritanian authorities often make migrants cross the border river at night, on makeshift canoes. On the other bank, the Senegalese Red Cross, funded by its Spanish counterpart, then takes charge of moving them on again.' Clandestine movement across borders, the European bugbear, is now part of a refoulement programme in the global South, approved by Brussels. The forward border has adverse repercussions, too, for Cen-Sad, a tentative community of Sahel-Saharan states proposing freedom of movement for goods, money and people, despite war on the Chad/Sudan frontier and many other obstacles, to which the EU has added by sponsoring deportations between Cen-Sad member states.

Finally there is the versatile character of irregular migration. Libya's willingness to shut down clandestine routes in its jurisdiction meant that, until the uprising in Tunisia last year, many fewer people were entering Italy – just as the numbers in the Canaries dropped after Frontex deployed in 2006. The result, however, was that by 2009 by far the largest numbers of irregular migrants entering the EU were coming via Greece: tens of thousands a year, mostly by land, across the Evros River from Turkey, but also by sea. Increasingly they were rerouting from the Maghreb and even sub-Saharan Africa: last year, a West African fixer in Istanbul told Voice of America that people-smuggling in the city was 'big business'. But closing off one route and forcing migrants down another tends to expose them to even greater dangers, and the Evros can be as treacherous as the open sea. In 2010, sixteen people drowned in the river in a single incident. UNHCR reported that most were thought to be Somalis. A Nigerian who set out in a party from Turkey in 2011 realised in short order that few of his fellow travellers could swim and no one else knew how to paddle an inflatable dinghy. The bedraggled group were arrested in Greece and sent back to Turkey.

Effective, radical border reinforcement might just be possible with enough money and personnel. It would boost European job creation by shifting thousands of unemployed people, from Finland to Hungary, into frontier security: maintenance crews for high-tech fences, coastguards, primary healthcare workers, paramilitaries, rendition squads, all-purpose janitors and bouncers, plus large numbers of low-skilled workers involved in the building of barracks for management and muscle on the front line. Construction alone could generate an ambitious public works project, with funding and tenders awarded in Brussels. Greece might even receive special disbursements for a restaging of the Persian Wars on the banks of the Evros: it is already building a twelve-kilometre fence in the area, where Frontex registered 40,000 irregular migrants in 2011. Yet the fully militarised model, which is underway on the US-Mexican frontier, is no use to the Europeans, whose land border, at nearly 9,000 kilometres, is three times as long. Then there is the matter of the European coastal frontier: another 42,000 kilometres. Can a community intent on rekindling its family values at the hearthside really hope to succeed while in charge of such a rambling estate?

Where border enforcement fails, there is always the rearguard option of destroying migrant camps. Greece, Italy and France have seen most of the action here. For several years in Italy, the target has been the Roma, and last December, the wish to tear these places down – more an impulse than a policy – culminated in a mob attack on a camp in a suburb of Turin after an accusation of rape. In Greece, there have been recent raids in Patras, in the northern Peloponnese: one on a cardboard camp, destroyed by riot police and bulldozers; another on an old textile factory, where police made a round of arrests and then set fire to the migrants' belongings, including clothes and temporary residence permits. Further north, near Igoumenitsa, between fifty and 100 illegal migrants were arrested in a forest camp near the ferry terminal: the camp was destroyed.

The best-known closure of a migrant camp occurred in 2002, when Nicolas Sarkozy, then the interior minister, ordered the evacuation of the Red Cross facility at Sangatte near Calais, after pressure from the British. Some 67,000 migrants, most of them asylum seekers, had found shelter in the Eurotunnel warehouse in Sangatte between 1999 and the day it shut. The demolition was completed in 2003: numbers of new arrivals in the UK were already falling. The destruction of the centre was a relief for New Labour, whose support for high levels of immigration was only acceptable to the press in exchange for a hard line on would-be asylum seekers. But the rubble of Sangatte also offered symbolic respite for France. The numbers piling up at the Channel crossing had been an embarrassment: bound for Britain, none of them wanted to claim asylum in France and the French didn't want to grant it.

Irregular migrants are no longer so conspicuous in northern France, but they are still a presence. If they congregate for too long in one place and numbers become too high, the bulldozers rumble out again with an infantry of riot police, as they did in 2009: the target on that occasion was the Jungle, an informal camp which, at the height of its notoriety, held more than 600 people, sleeping under plastic sheeting. There were 278 arrests at the time of the demolition; at least half were of minors.

There is no proof that breaking up camps deters newcomers. If you have someone to show you, you can find around a dozen 'squats' and 'jungles' in Nord-Pas-de-Calais, where prospective Channel-crossers camp rough in sparse stands of trees on the edge of industrial estates, or slivers of woodland between a main road and a field. Further east there are minimalist camps on the motorway, where migrants haunt the rest areas, watching trucks pull in. Numbers in the department, at any given time, would be between one and three hundred.

Thousands of Kosovans still claim asylum in France every year, but at the end of the 1990s the figures were much higher and accounted for a good proportion of those in Sangatte. Nowadays along the Channel seaboard, you come across Iraqis, Afghans, Eritreans, Sudanese, Ethiopians and Somalis. The protagonists have changed and the statistics are less dramatic, but Mathieu Quinette, who runs the Médecins du Monde office in Dunkirk, believes that a decade of clandestine migration to Britain has seen 'tens of thousands' of successful crossings since the camp in Sangatte was razed.

Nonetheless, people can wait for a very long time and life has become harder for the migrants. Their camps are regularly destroyed, their sleeping bags and blankets burned by the police.

People whose fingerprints were taken on their way into France through another EU country – French police can check this on the Eurodac fingerprint database – will often be deposited across the border. Sometimes they will be bussed back to the country concerned (unless it was Greece, which the EU agrees has too much on its plate); sometimes released after a spell in local detention. Survivors return and rebuild, and the process begins again. Their little woodland refuges are isolated; in the absence of the Red Cross hangar, which gave structure and rhythm to their waiting game, there has been a rise in microwars between gangs of smugglers and groups of migrants. Lay-bys and rest areas have sometimes been in fierce contention, with Vietnamese groups fending off Russian and Chechen gangs, and Eritreans battling with Kurdish smugglers. The growth of parasitic crime, on the back of unauthorised entry, is a price that France may have to pay for ensuring that the *sans-papiers* along the Channel coast are kept out of the public eye.

All the same, UNHCR figures show that in 2010 the highest number of asylum applications in Europe, around 50,000, was lodged in France. In 2011 that figure rose to 60,000. Most applicants are from Asia and the Balkans. But in Calais I met a group from Darfur who were in Libya at the time of the uprising and made a terrified exit to Europe. One of them, A., had just been evicted from what's known as Africa House, a deserted industrial building near another deserted industrial building which the authorities smashed up in 2010 because it was the site of the previous incarnation of Africa House: the trials of statelessness in Calais tend to repeat themselves.

Matters could get no worse, A. felt, if he lodged his asylum claim in France. 'How did you enter Libya in the first place?' a retired accountant volunteering for Secours Catholique asked, as we filled out the young man's application in a set of prefab huts a few hundred yards from a scruffy British booze emporium. He'd crossed the frontier on a camel, he told us. The congenial accountant, it seemed to me, could already hear the laughter at the sous-préfecture. 'Right,' he said, with a look of resolve, 'I think we'll just put "truck".' A. has no connections in France and doesn't speak the language, but he has escaped from a country where to be black and foreign was a life-endangering condition and applied to live in another where it is simply a disadvantage, which is a step forward, even by Europe's accounting.

For the moment we mainly hear the din of battle, between the painstaking communitarian ideal and the forces of cosmopolitanism. Struggling up a Mediterranean beach to claim asylum after an epic journey is a powerful statement. So is the electric fence. But tens of thousands of prosperous, qualified people are also on this frontline, because byzantine visa regimes are denying them entry to EU countries. Managers who cannot hire the personnel they need are in the thick of it too. Last year a British Asian running a software engineering firm in the City told me he'd lost heart trying to apply to the Home Office for short-stay business visas for colleagues from abroad, and given up completely on work permits for software geeks. He is now a regular outsourcer to India.

Europe's tight immigration policy also brings its humanitarian pretensions into question: the holding camps, the charter flights with deportees in restraint positions, the virtual frontier creeping inexorably beyond the geographical border. All these, and the fact that more than 15,000 people have died in the last twenty years trying to circumvent European entry restrictions, cast doubt on the idea that European values, reinvigorated after World War Two, are synonymous with universal rights. The oddity is that many of the people who are refused entry have affirmed their faith in those values and reiterated those rights by making the journey in the first place. Can rights and values be universal if they seem, even after lengthy explanations of the communitarian case, to be rationed by a subset of rules about sovereign boundaries? Perhaps we should agree to think of rights and values as limited resources, and admit that Europe is now caught in a bitter struggle over who can or can't access them.

The outcome of that struggle is less obvious than it seems. Plenty of people are disturbed by the consequences of European immigration policy, whatever they think of the principles. In France, when the Interior ministry began detaining illegal immigrant children at the school gate in 2006, there was a surge in political fostering by indigenous families. Dozens of French children acquired temporary siblings, as their parents took in threatened minors. This radical solidarity prefers the moral case over any argument about national borders. In France, the deportation of Jews in the 1940s is still a vivid precedent.

A thin blue line of European technocrats and civil servants defends immigration as an answer to Europe's ageing demographic profile, the doubtful future of pension provision and the shortage of indigenous unskilled labour. The door must be kept open, in this view, whatever politicians and the popular press have to say. For this group, principle is neither here nor there: outcomes are everything.

Libertarian elites firmly believe that the dust of protectionism should vanish behind vast columns of goods, services, capital and human beings moving freely around the world. This is both a principle and, it seems, a matter of expediency: they are quick to complain about the shortage of qualified labour on the nearest corner and go on to argue that a stream of unskilled, exploitable workers is necessary to maintain the local infrastructure on which they happen to depend if they're to arrive at the office in functioning cabs on serviceable roads.

And so to the mystery of ordinary citizens. European views on immigration are mostly negative. According to an Ipsos poll of 17,000 respondents in twenty-three countries last summer, Europeans tend to feel that there are too many migrants and they congest public services. Many believe they are competing for jobs, despite evidence to the contrary. Migrants are not the enemy exactly, but they threaten to disrupt the orderly world we have struggled so hard to create, in which we stand a little lifelessly like the model citizens of a Lego village, everyone in his place, all of us transacting in our button currency. When asked to consider why human beings move in ever greater numbers, we shake our heads stiffly from side to side, as we did for the last research poll and the one before that. We grasp that migrants may be poor yet fail to see that more prosperity in the global south would probably mean more migration. And not necessarily to Europe, which might one day be competing for immigrants with countries such as Turkey or Brazil as patterns of human movement change. 'In the future,' the migration scholar Hein de Haas believes, 'the question will no longer be how to prevent migrants from coming, but how to attract them.'

Still, from time to time we come to life and look around with a fresh eye. Another poll, conducted by Ipsos/Mori, commissioned by the Migration Observatory and published last September, suggests that British opposition to newcomers is lower, on the whole, in areas where immigrants have settled than it is elsewhere. The exception, oddly, is Scotland – a low immigration area – where 20 per cent of respondents would like to see more migrants. London thinks immigration should remain at current levels. In the Midlands and Wales, a narrow majority feels that immigration should be reduced 'a lot', and in the UK as a whole, 60 per cent or more believe the figures need to fall. But the point here is how much more widespread anti-immigration sentiment might have been, given this long moment of recession, and the strength of nativist sentiment, everywhere in Europe, in the face of globalisation. During the 1960s and 1970s, when immigration was a good deal lower than it is now, a series of surveys found a far greater percentage of Britons opposed to immigrants. Multiculturalism had something to teach us after all.

4

America is irresistible. Nothing to do with choosing.

Richard Rodriguez, *Days of Obligation*

Migration is said to be good for host cultures. Geographers, demographers and business people believe it is, especially in the US, where one migrant group after another – Jews, Poles, Italians, Irish – has auditioned for a role in the great musical of American identity. The competition has been bitter, especially between newcomers and predecessors, and the typecasting has been crude, yet sooner or later every minority earns its place in the chorus. Nonetheless there's a growing sense in some parts of the US that enough is enough, the stage is full to capacity and the show can no longer go on as it has. The source of this impatience is illegal immigration from Mexico, which is no longer seen primarily as a supply of service employees, farm labourers and building workers, but as a threat to an indebted nation still embroiled in distant wars, with land borders to north and south that it can't patrol as effectively as it would like and unemployment hovering at around 9 per cent. The US already has more than eleven million unauthorised migrants. About six and a half million are from Mexico and another two million from other parts of Latin America. Every year, many thousands more are crossing from Mexico without permission, to swell their ranks. Roughly 500,000 Hispanics – 8 per cent of the population of the state – are living in Arizona without authorisation. Arizona has become an operational front in yet another desert conflict.

The battle against illegal migration is a domestic version of America's interventions overseas, with many of the same trappings: big manpower commitments, militarisation, pursuit, detection, rendition, loss of life. The Mexican border was already the focus of attention before 9/11; it is now a fixation that shows no signs of abating even as Obama draws down the numbers abroad. Despite war-weariness at home, war has remained the model for curbing illegal immigration; territorial integrity and the preservation of national identity are the goals. Unlike the invasion of Iraq, this is a respectable struggle – all nation states assert the right to secure borders. Yet watertight security is becoming harder to achieve as the global era brings new pressures to bear on the frontier, adding to the older challenge posed by people wishing to move freely. At fortified boundaries, frailty lurks beneath the show of strength.

The tough stance on the US southern border is fuelling bitter animosities. It endorses the north-south divide between two continents and two big economies, and gives offence in Mexico, where the northerly movement of undocumented people is seen as a vital form of exchange for both countries. Political liberals in the US tend to agree on this, seeing the benefits to Mexicans and the families they support from abroad. So do corporate boards and chambers of commerce, whose members celebrate migrant labour, on or off the books: that's business at the price of immigration control. Then there are the ultras, market liberals who favour greater freedom of human movement, in step with the boundless mobility of capital: that's business at all costs, above and beyond the petty constraints of sovereignty. But conservatives in the South-West don't like what they're seeing and in Arizona they have drafted state laws on illegal immigration that vex the federal courts and alienate the business communities while raising local tension between Hispanics and whites. Over the last ten years, beefed-up border control has led to many more deaths among migrants, forcing them to find alternative routes through remote desert in their quest for a livelihood. But it's not clear whether punitive legislation and warlike methods of enforcement strengthen the frontier or whether they turn manageable disorder into a disaster.

The border with Mexico stretches for nearly 2,000 miles. Much of that is underwritten by the Rio Grande, but as natural barriers go, the river is less formidable than the wilderness either side of the frontier. The harsh Sonoran Desert in the south-western borderlands runs deep into Arizona, and into the defensive imagination of a white majority who take it as a God-given affirmation of the integrity of their state, and of the United States itself. A magnificent and costly border wall – 'the fence', 'the barrier' – now runs in sections, like a work by Christo and Jeanne-Claude, along parts of the frontier, but the terrain in most of Arizona is so fierce that it was thought until recently to be a stronger disincentive to illegal entry than any man-made obstacle.

Border vigilance in its present form took shape in the 1990s under the first Clinton administration. In 1993 the Border Patrol in Texas reacted to large numbers of illegal crossings near El Paso with high-profile reinforcement. Operation Gatekeeper, designed to stem illegal migrant flows at San Diego, followed in California. Army surplus landing mats, dating from Vietnam, were stood on their ends to build a short stretch of wall along the border, where more than half a million 'illegal aliens' had been apprehended the previous year. People could cut holes in the steel panels or climb them – there were useful toe and handholds – but the wall put an end to cars and pickups going across and set up a physical marker between north and south. As it grew, it transformed a line defined by international treaty, a few dusty frontier posts, cattle barriers and rolls of barbed wire, into a monumental declaration of intent. Numbers of illegal entries fell sharply around El Paso in the east and San Diego in the west, leaving a broad migrant channel in the intervening stretch of borderland. Many Latin Americans were ready to try it, especially after Mexico devalued the peso in 1994. At that stage crossing the wilderness wasn't the only option for a clandestine migrant, but matters were moving fast and in 2006, the US Congress passed the Secure Fence Act, requiring 700 miles of built deterrence: not a wall as such, but a series of extended barriers along stretches of the border. The landing mats looked footling by comparison.

By 2010 Arizona had at least 125 miles of high fencing and about 180 miles of vehicle barriers. Determined migrants could still get across, and by now it was apparent that the desert was not doing all that it should to keep out the enemy. Border towns were among the first places to be reinforced and security has been upgraded since. There are two crossings, for instance, between Nogales, Arizona and Nogales, Mexico. The aged fencing at the downtown crossing, weakened by wear and tear, including tunnelling, was replaced this year. The Mariposa crossing, on the outskirts of town, is mainly a transit point for heavy goods, where articulated trucks back up for half a mile or more on the US side, an endless line of upright exhaust pipes beside a verge of sand, scrub and trash. This, too, is undergoing a major overhaul, largely to cope with the volume of traffic, but security is being tightened as well. Mariposa is the preferred point of deportation for illegal migrants: truck drivers, unlike the crowds of tourists at the downtown crossing, are used to the sight of captives being herded into Mexico like livestock.

In the view from the Arizona state capitol, human smuggling and drug smuggling are intimately connected. During a gubernatorial debate in 2010, Jan Brewer, the Republican governor, said of undocumented migrants: 'The majority of them in my opinion and I think in the opinion of law enforcement … are not coming here to work. They are coming here, and they're bringing drugs.' But how does this hold up under scrutiny? It is true that many of the men profiting from human smuggling, with their millionaire ranches on the edges of the cities in northern Mexico, are making bigger amounts from drugs. Take Nogales (Mexico) again. In terms of cartel geography, it belongs to a generous swathe of territory worked by the Sinaloa cartel. There were clashes in 2010 with rival cartels (the remnants of the Beltrán Leyva brothers' cartel and the paramilitary group Los Zetas), but drugs continue to cross the border and some, it is also true, are carried by unauthorised migrants: people who don't have the money for their passage can repay the debt by acting as mules, delivering packages to safe houses in the US. But the carrying capacity of a foot-slogger is no match for a commercial trailer, or the hydraulic arm of a tow truck, or a hidden compartment in an outsize SUV. The impressive quantities of narcotics confiscated along the US-Mexican border in 2009–10 (three million kilos of marijuana, cocaine, heroin and other drugs) and the drainage of weapons from the US into Mexico (6,800 seized en route in the same year) tell us less about the vices of the undocumented migrant than they do about sophisticated smuggling operations, North American drug preferences, the effect of prohibition and the promiscuity of gun culture.

Unlike Brewer, Border Patrol staff believe that fewer than 10 per cent of the people they catch coming across have criminal intentions. The figures contradict her too. If drugs are the reason migrants infiltrate the border, why are there so many apprehensions of 'illegals' (170,000 in the Tucson Sector from October 2009 to June 2010, for instance) and so few federal prosecutions in the state on drugs charges (1,107 in the same period)? How is it that out of the half-million undocumented Hispanics in Arizona, fewer than 3,000 are in state penitentiaries on drug offences? Why, in Pima County, a frontline border county which includes Tucson, do crime figures for 2010 published by the sheriff's office show incidents involving 'controlled substances' running at lower rates than fraud, criminal damage or burglary, and only slightly higher than drunk driving?

Drugs or no drugs, unauthorised migration puts pressure on the border, and since 9/11 the crackle of vigilance has grown steadily louder as federal, state and county resources pour in to check a threat that is ill-defined in reality but which, like the spectre of WMD in Iraq, achieves high resolution in the eyes of policy-makers. Among the various agencies hovering over 'border issues' in Arizona are US Immigration and Customs Enforcement (ICE), US Customs and Border Protection, the Federal Emergency Management Agency (Fema), the DEA, the FBI, the Arizona Department of Public Safety and the sheriffs' offices of several counties, including Maricopa. More than 500

National Guard reservists were sent to Arizona in 2010 and should have left in September: the redeployment is on hold. A move is afoot in Washington to increase Border Patrol staff, now roughly 20,000, by a further 5,000 in the next four years and to deploy 6,000 National Guard along the length of the frontier. The bill is sponsored by John McCain (Arizona), who, like George W. Bush, was once an immigration liberal but sees where the votes have come to lie in recent years.

Two highly visible protagonists in the immigration drama, Salvador Reza and the Republican state senator, Russell Pearce, embody the tensions in Arizona almost to the point of caricature. In February 2011, Reza, a Latino community leader in Phoenix, was detained in the downtown county jail. His offence was not wholly clear. The trouble began the previous day while he'd been in an overflow room at the state capitol listening in as a senate committee debated a bill to crack down on undocumented migrants. The gist of the bill was to make life impossible for anyone in Arizona without papers: impossible to drive a car, or enrol a child in school, or be treated at a hospital for non-emergency care. Any infant born to an undocumented migrant would acquire a docket stating that it was not a US citizen. The presence of one undocumented person in a rent-paying household would mean the landlord had to evict them all. Reza, a large man in his sixties, with silver hair in a ponytail and a walrus moustache, was applauding arguments against the bill from opponents in committee.

Pearce, the president of the State Senate and the driving force behind the legislation, was furious and told security that in future Reza should not be allowed into the capitol buildings. When Reza arrived the following day for a meeting, he was told to leave; there was a scuffle; he and a fellow activist were arrested. Though he's a US citizen, Reza is a pantomime monster for worried conservatives in Arizona, just as Pearce is for Hispanics and liberal whites. Pearce is a fifth-generation Arizonan, and a stickler for law and order, border law in particular. He comes to the point a fraction too soon and has no time for nuance; the fine interpretation of a law and its violation are much the same in his view and, oddly for a legislator, he won't agree that if it's unenforceable, it's of very little use to anyone. He parries accusations of racism with the assertion that the law is colour-blind, which only adds to his villainy in the eyes of his enemies. He is a broad-shouldered, powerful man, in his sixties like Reza, who speaks in well-formed sentences that aren't quite sound bites; he has a thick, acrylic complexion, like a work in progress left on the easel overnight.

Pearce announced when we met that he had never been against immigration, only illegal immigration: what's 'not to understand' about the word 'illegal'? He followed with some terse thoughts on race: 'I don't care what colour it is, as long as it's American.' Business people who were opposed to his stance, he said, were mostly the ones who acted unfairly, outside the law, driving down their own labour costs and cheating honest competitors. This was a kind of theft – 'I don't support stealing, though I see it benefits the thief and his family' – and it displaced American workers (the figures are always hotly debated but they suggest 'illegals' do indeed compete with high-school drop-outs in the job market). 'It's embarrassing,' he added, 'and anti-American.' He deplored the loss of tax revenue and social security contributions, even though many undocumented aliens file tax returns and still more have social security payments deducted at source, under a false social security number, or someone else's, which means that they pay in but will never be able to claim. The sums come out differently depending on the accounting, but Pearce sticks to his headline findings that illegal immigrants are a net loss to government and besides, as he reminded me, the law, not the money, is the bottom line. 'Take the handcuffs off of law enforcement,' he said with the ghost of a gleam in his battle-hardened eye.

Several hours after Reza was arrested at the capitol buildings, his supporters were crowded round another monitor, in the county court in Phoenix, which doubles as a jailhouse, waiting to hear whether he would get out and what charges, if any, would be brought. I was in the building, crammed against a TouchPay banking machine for transfers to prisoners ('a fast, secure, convenient way to deposit money into inmate accounts ... Mastercard or Visa'). An anti-anti-immigration senator cut a furrow through the room and addressed a sterling defence of Reza to the nearest news camera. The feeling among the crowd, largely Latino, was that Pearce had blackballed Reza from the state capitol, that the charge would be trespass and that this would probably violate the First Amendment. In a whisper, but hardly in confidence, a young Latino lawyer told me: 'They want to de-*tain* his ass.' Reza was released later that night, along with his colleague, pending a court appearance. On the steps of the 4th Avenue jail he assumed a statuesque pose, legs apart, plaid shirt filling in the breeze, and denounced 'a level of repression I have never seen before'. Arizona, he said, 'has to come back into civilisation'. Huddled in the chilly night air, the crowd applauded. The younger activist detained with him had put up a fight, been manhandled by security at the capitol buildings, and dragged out by the hair. A journalist asked her for a contact number but she'd used her cell phone to film the fracas and it had been confiscated.

In Roberto Bolaño's novel *2666*, a talk-show host on Tijuana TV interviews a doomed cross-border veteran who holds 'the record for most expulsions from the United States': he is a scapegoat for the failures of the Mexican economy, the second largest in Latin America, who keeps returning, unbidden, from the wilderness in which he was supposed to disappear. 'Do you know how many times he had entered the United States illegally? Three hundred and forty-five!' After the fiftieth crossing, we're told, a heartfelt sympathy set in and the smugglers stopped charging him. On subsequent crossings he became a magical asset: better to have him in the group, because if anyone were to be caught, it was sure to be him. The talk-show host asks if he means to keep on trying. 'Trying what?' the man says. This mythic figure, steeped in heroic absurdity, is worth remembering as you stand at the border in the dust storm of deterrence that makes it hard to see to the other side, where national sovereignty means little to people impoverished by fate or political economy. The other figure to bear in mind is this:

for every illegal migrant apprehended, Border Patrol estimates that three get across.

In Arizona, the pursuit of aliens is no longer confined to a costly cat and mouse game along the frontier. It is a grim paper chase that takes place in traffic queues and metered parking zones in Phoenix, the kitchens of fast-food restaurants, mechanics' workshops and building sites miles from the fence. Oscar, a fluent English-speaker in his thirties, was not the symbolic serial offender imagined by Bolaño, but he had a sobering story to tell about the new crack-down, what it was to attempt the border and how it felt to fail. I found him stacking cans of peeled tomatoes by a portable gas stove, in a tent shelter just across the frontier in Nogales set up by a US-Mexican migrant-support NGO. He had been holed up in Mexico for months, having lived in the US, been expelled and crossed back over several times, only to be caught and returned. Oscar's misery began in 2005, when it was discovered that his immigration documents were not in order. He'd opted for volun-tary departure – a dismal alternative to detention or unaffordable lawsuits – and then crept back in. Subsequently, in Phoenix, he'd run up a couple of parking fines and paid them off using a fake ID. He'd let the third one slide, and wound up in an ICE detention facility for three months for illegal entry, before being deposited in Nogales. Not long afterwards he came back through the down-town crossing and managed to remain in the US for three years, until he was nailed on a traffic offence, sent to a detention facility in Arizona and deported again.

Oscar was not a man to hang around. Within days he'd joined a party of migrants, led by a coyote, or paid guide, on a venture into the Sonoran Desert. It was a three-day walk from the fron-tier to their pick-up point. He was flayed below the knees by cacti and when his shoes came to pieces – the shoes he'd been given in prison in Arizona – he walked the last day barefoot over red rock, a coarse oxidised sandstone. In Tucson he discovered that the soles of each foot had become a single blister, from ball to heel, like a gel pack. He was deported again and on his next attempt, shortly afterwards, he and his companions were spotted by Border Patrol.

During the chase he lost his food and water. He survived for two days (it was October) and eventually made it to Phoenix. Soon enough he got on the wrong side of a drugs bust – his brother-in-law's marijuana was found in his car, he claimed – and he was deported yet again. The refuge by the border post where a dozen indigent, would-be migrants hung in the shade with a listless posse of dogs, was now the long and short of it for Oscar. He'd been using crack, he admitted, but had managed to shake the habit: his suppressed rage and the look of convertible longing in his eyes – a longing for his family, or maybe his earlier life, or maybe a proscribed substance – made you wonder if he was telling the truth.

In fact the difficulty for Oscar had arisen very much earlier, when the family lawyer had failed to sort out his paperwork in the 1990s. The deeper problem still was that his family had brought him to Chicago in the mid-1980s, when he was three. He had a wife, an ex by now, and three young daughters with US citizenship living in Arizona, where he had worked as a courier, a line manager at a fast-food chain and a damp-course expert. He knew everyone and their grandmother in Phoenix. In Mexico his circle of acquaintance was probably confined to a handful of drug-users, dealers, human smugglers and deportees. His cheerful, busy friend Ricardo, who breezed in while Oscar was telling his story, had been pulled in for jaywalking in Phoenix in 2009. He'd shown the police his papers from the Mexican Consulate and a student ID – he was enrolled to study architecture – but he was handed over to ICE and chose voluntary deportation over a spell in federal detention. Ricardo was twenty-four. He'd been nearly two years in limbo when we met. He'd been brought to the US at an earlier age even than Oscar – he was one year old – and had almost no family connections in Mexico. Oscar and Ricardo were Mexican on paper, but cast adrift in an unfamiliar environment they were closer to what Hannah Arendt and her generation would have described as *apatrides*.

Phoenix lay under a dull sky. It was early morning, with few signs of life, when we left. We picked up State Route 85 at Buckeye and headed south through a magnificent valley strewn with saguaro and palo verde; after an hour or more we passed the Barry M. Goldwater Air Force Range, a test site for dummy ordnance. I was making for the borderlands again and before long my companions would be putting out water supplies on desert routes where migrants were known to travel and known to have died. Liana Rowe took a hand off the wheel and gestured at the bombing range. There were no water stations there, she said, because the military had refused permission. 'Really,' one of the volunteers in the back said with deadpan sarcasm. 'But we know people come through there,' Rowe went on. Another hour and we were on the outskirts of Ajo, an old copper settlement, where the pale terraced workings rose in the near distance like the remains of an abstruse civilisation. When the mines opened during World War One they generated a surge of Mexican migrant labour, but extraction ended in the 1980s and now the place is solemn and still, though the area is part of the regular beat for Border Patrol.

In May 2001, among dozens of crossings, a group of twenty-six migrants entered the Tucson Sector from Mexico. During a vigorous pursuit by Border Patrol, fourteen lost their bearings, including three guides, ending up in a stretch of desert known as the Devil's Highway, where they died. They were not the first casualties since Operation Gatekeeper but this was the highest number of recorded deaths in a single incident and pointed up the human consequences of the security drive at the border, where undocumented migrants had been moving back and forth in relative safety for decades.

The deaths were a scandal on both sides of the frontier. By then a group of activists in Tucson had already formed Humane Borders, an NGO seeking to 'reduce the number of migrants dying in the desert' and advocating secure legal status for undocumented immigrants. Rowe, an ordained minister in the United Church of Christ, is the Phoenix co-ordinator of the organisation, one of many support and solidarity groups that sprang up in Arizona as a result of tightened border policy. Her work, she explained, was a legacy of the Sanctuary movement of the early 1980s, when churches in the US brought refugees from the wars in El Salvador and Guatemala to safety north of the border, in a modern version of the nineteenth-century Underground Railroad. Arizona had played a prominent part in this movement. 'Sanctuary activists could see what was going to happen as the urban crossings were sealed off,' Rowe said, referring to San Diego and El Paso, and events confirmed their misgivings.

Humane Borders and others have compiled a painstaking log of migrant deaths in the Sonoran Desert, with information from the medical examiners' offices, Border Patrol and the Mexican Consulate. Geographers have taken the data and expressed them as a map of the frontier area, studded with red dots, each representing at least one death inside the US. The dots are so densely grouped in places that you might be looking at lumpfish caviar. A ten-year retrospective 'deaths map', covering the period 1999–2009, charts 1,755 deaths. 'They were wrong,' Rowe said as she ran through the figures, 'about the desert putting people off.' The primary purpose of the deaths map is not to alert the world to the fate of desperate or adventurous people, but to give Rowe and her colleagues an idea where to set out water: after careful extrapolations from the map and tough negotiations with landowners, private and public, Humane Borders has established water stations in dozens of locations in the middle of nowhere.

At a depot in the Organ Pipe Cactus National Monument, a Unesco 'biosphere reserve', Rowe switched the car for a flatbed truck loaded with five-gallon bottles, a large container of water and two wheelbarrows, drove it out to the first water station, parked the truck, filled the bottles and had us wheel them to the station, a distance from the road, where we topped up a barrel. She checked the tap and ran a chlorine test. The volunteers, probation officers in the Phoenix area who were bitterly opposed to the crackdown on undocumented migrants, picked up a bit of litter – someone had been here – and we moved on to the next station to repeat the process. Litter dumped in nature reserves by exhausted migrants counts against them in the eyes of hard-line environmentalists, and their bodies are only slightly more acceptable. Some people say

Humane Borders is complicit in illegal migration, Rowe remarked. 'Because we put out water. That's a refusal to see what drives them across in the first place.'

We secured the wheelbarrows and bottles on the tailboard, drove to the depot and put away the truck. On the way back in Rowe's car, she spoke at length about the harsh new conditions facing migrants. She evoked an earlier age, when clandestine migration was mostly 'a mom, pop and donkey operation'; you could almost glimpse the Flight into Egypt, restaged with plaster figurines in the crypt of a Mexican church – for a long moment I'd forgotten Rowe was a devout Christian. Border vigilance had raised the stakes, she went on, attracting new, high-powered Mexican smugglers who looked for wide profit margins (the going rate for a crossing that starts in Guatemala is around $7,000). A cottage industry has been transformed into a lucrative business whose clients are forced to part with far more money than previous generations paid, for a far more dangerous crossing. Homeland Security, Rowe argued, has burnished the dollar signs in the eyes of the drug cartels, driven up the costs for migrants and introduced a death penalty clause into their ordeal by forcing them through remote desert. 'If you're going to quote me, please don't refer to me as Reverend Rowe. Or Reverend anything.' The skies had cleared, the sun was behind us, and the desert city of Phoenix, where she would preach the next morning, rose ahead like a landlocked Dubai.

On the morning of 11 August 2010, Angélica Martínez was working in a restaurant in Phoenix when police raided it, searching for undocumented migrants. She was removed to a detention facility outside town and appeared in court in the evening. She raised the money for a bond and was released the following day. In September she was sentenced and spent three weeks in Estrella Women's Jail in Phoenix, under the jurisdiction of the Maricopa County sheriff, going from there into the charge of Immigration and Customs Enforcement (ICE), at a federal detention centre where she spent another three and a half months. This is normally the prelude to deportation, but Angélica was able to remain by filing a lawsuit whose outcome, when I met her early in 2011, looked uncertain. She has been in the US since 1999: 'I came in a car with my daughter and another family. My son was born here.' She has worked for most of that time in the service sector. It's not clear that the family is a net loss to the state of Arizona, as Russell Pearce's version has it: what Angélica parts with in sales taxes in a year outstrips what she might have paid in income tax, always assuming she was paid off the books, in cash (but, to repeat, millions of working 'illegals' make tax and social security contributions). Her children will eventually become able-bodied adults, who can launder the clothes, tend the lawns and flip the burgers of their fellow Arizonans at competitive rates. Angélica's son is a US citizen but his mother has no papers; neither does his sister.

Angélica is typical of the new, urban offender invented by the culture of pursuit and prosecution in cities a good distance from the frontier, where people of different ethnic and national origins, one group with the power to drive legislation, the other with the impertinence to resist, are increasingly at odds. This conflict has been building for a while: Latino activists identify a key moment in 2000, when Arizona passed a law ending bilingual teaching in schools in favour of segregated classes with special English immersion for Spanish-speakers. Opponents of the legislation claimed that it was wrong – and prejudicial to their chances – to stream immigrant pupils into language learning when they should be mastering the curriculum. Border discipline in the state had already hardened and there was a growing suspicion of Hispanics, who read the law as a deliberate affront. Then, in 2004, the state legislature made it a crime for public service employees to fail to report undocumented migrants and obliged anyone handling social security benefits to verify the legal status of applicants. Raids on workplaces increased and traffic offences soon spiralled into 'illegal alien' cases. Looking back over the legislation, a Hispanic activist in Phoenix told me, people felt they should have seen it coming. Whites, he thought, were better at anticipating trouble: when it was clear that Hispanic children might shortly be a majority in kindergarten and primary schools – they're currently 42 per cent and rising – the threatened majority, already concerned about Hispanics taking too many jobs, had reacted fast. The 2004 legislation, in his eyes, was proof of their alacrity.

In 2008 the Legal Arizona Workers Act increased pressure on companies to hire within the law and check the status of potential employees on E-Verify, a Homeland Security system on the Internet. More than 90,000 Latinos left the state in the following two years; the number of waged Hispanic employees fell by about 56,000 and the number of 'self-employed' rose by 25,000. The Public Policy Institute of California, which crunched the numbers, argued convincingly that these trends were not driven by recession. But it was legislation in 2010 that felt to Hispanics like a declaration of war. Senate Bill 1070, as it was known, proposed a federal responsibility for local law enforcers, who would now be able to check the papers of anyone they had already stopped for a separate offence, typically a traffic infringement. In essence, the law formalised the growing reality of workplace raids and selective vehicle checks. It made the federal offence of unauthorised immigration into a state crime: Arizona was about to become a stop-and-detain jurisdiction.

Like the 'no bilingualism in schools' ruling, SB1070 brought many legal residents and US citizens of Hispanic origin across the stepped divide that normally separates 'legals' and 'illegals' in migrant communities everywhere: it seemed to both to have a punitive, ethnic edge. Migrant rights groups call it 'hate legislation'. The spirit of the law drew fire from Washington and cursory criticism from Obama; the letter of the law met with opposition from the federal courts – and injunctions on four counts. Through 2012, as the Supreme Court deliberated the larger question of whether Arizona's new legislation was not pre-empted by federal law, the provision in SB1070 allowing a local police inquiry on a specific offence to evolve into a demand for documents was blocked. But in June, the court decided not to strike it down even while ruling against three other provisions. Pearce was delighted and felt the 'most compelling piece' of his legislation had been upheld. In theory there is no mission creep when a migrant is pulled over for running a red light. Local law enforcement sets little store by theory, however, and Arizona is now officially a 'papers please' culture, rolling inexorably towards racial profiling in the view of its critics: a rogue state at the margins of the Union.

The bill had met with stiff resistance from the outset. In 2010 opponents across the country decided on a boycott, which had been their riposte in the late 1980s when Arizona baulked at the Martin Luther King holiday. After SB1070, a group of California truckers refused to work in the state, the mayor of San Francisco advised his employees to avoid visiting and by 2011, dozens of valuable conference bookings had been stood down. Money and contracts have been veering away ever since and many business-people who oppose the laws admit that it's difficult to separate the mounting damage done by the boycott from the lingering effects of the financial crisis in 2008, which dealt a shattering blow to the construction industry where many Hispanics work. The de facto boycott remained in place, as Latinos continued leaving the state for other parts of the US: many families are still eyeing up the possibility. Others, separated by a deportation, have already opted for upheaval and poverty – reunion in any case – by moving to Mexico (not 'back' to Mexico, because often this is their first journey outside the US). If Angélica's luck runs out, she and her children will have to consider this possibility.

The latest bill, the one Reza had disparaged at the state capitol, is even more incendiary in the eyes of Hispanics, which made it seem odd that this forceful character, often accused of anti-white prejudice by his enemies, hadn't played up the race angle on the steps of the 4th Avenue jail on the night of his release. Most activists and many Latinos are convinced that Arizona is in the grip of race hysteria: an idea hotly denied by Pearce and Governor Brewer. Alfredo Gutiérrez, a radical of Reza's generation who held a state senate seat in Arizona for nearly fifteen years, is outspoken about what he takes to be the racial component in this bitter struggle. Gutiérrez argues that 'Arizona is for immigration what Mississippi was for civil rights,' that 'the term "illegal immigration" stands for hatred of Mexicans' and that 'somewhere in this country the immigration debate may be about immigration, but not in Arizona.'

Reza and Gutiérrez both know about the language controversy in schools: as a boy in Texas, Reza says, he was beaten on the hands with a wooden board for speaking Spanish; in Arizona, Gutiérrez had his mouth taped up when he did the same. Both are highly eloquent, doubtless as a consequence, even if their approaches differ. Reza's militancy maps the immigration issue onto old indigenous land claims and cosmologies; I've seen him with conches, incense and totemic spears, summoning indigenous American ancestors in the grounds of the capitol building, before trudging onto the dreary stone concourse to demonstrate against Pearce's laws. Gutiérrez, for his part, isn't sure about the conches and totems – evidence in his eyes that the dubious appeal of faith and origin is on the rise, on one side as on the other. But he's not surprised that the history of the South-West, whether it's a religious nativist interpretation or a long-standing quarrel with nineteenth-century state formation in continental America, remains a mustering point for Latino activists.

Gutiérrez doesn't dismiss the old arguments out of hand. The fact that the US acquired so much territory administered or claimed by Mexico in the 1840s and 1850s – the whole of modern-day Texas, New Mexico, California, Arizona, Nevada, Utah, parts of Wyoming and Colorado – looms like unfinished business at the back of his conversation. But he is more intent on the recent history of migration. Gutiérrez was born in the US to Mexican parents. His father was deported in the 1930s under Hoover's forced repatriation programme and returned during World War Two to mine copper in Arizona. By then the US had turned away from repatriation and begun drafting in Mexican labour, mostly in agriculture, under the Bracero programme. The scheme would have ended in 1947, had it not been for pressure from US farmers to keep it going. There were still plenty of Mexican labourers in the country in the 1950s, including Gutiérrez Sr, and the processing of newcomers had grown relaxed, to say the least. But if the presence of 'illegals' was useful, it was also unsettling: Operation Wetback, a well-advertised eviction programme that threw roughly a million Mexicans back over the border in 1954, helped to allay the anxiety. People like Gutiérrez take a dim view of US immigration policy on the southern border. First you need us, then you don't. Much that has happened since the 1990s recalls the dark days of Operation Wetback.

Matters look even more troubling to anyone with doubts about the settlement of the US/Mexican frontier in the first place. There are around thirty-one million people of Mexican origin in the US and by no means all of them cling to a sense of old territorial injustice. In Arizona, however, the sense of a creeping reconquista – a Hispanic recovery of land lost in the course of US expansion – is the stuff of ultra-conservative fantasy. It rarely surfaces in migrant discourse, yet earlier this year, on the steps of the state assembly, a Hispanic fundamentalist shouted at a deputy from the Maricopa sheriff's office that he and his kind – which I took to mean Anglos – would soon be a minority in the state. And perhaps all the border states? I found myself thinking, as the words took on a bitter, coded resonance: it was systematic settlement by North Americans in the 1820s and 1830s, intended to outnumber Mexicans, that had paved the way to independence for Texas. At this remote edge of the ethnic political imagination, the Union's acquisition of so much land a century and a half ago, by war and purchase, remains a burning issue, despite the solemn ratifications and the money made over to the Mexican exchequer ($245 million in present-day terms for the last purchase, in 1853). Even level heads like Gutiérrez will invoke the territorial history in their defence of immigrants if you push hard enough. Unlawful movement across a frontier generates friction, and so do historic grievances. The border may have been upholstered and fortified since the 1990s, but these quarrels can reduce it to a cordon of frayed rope.

Arguments about freedom of movement are part of the wider controversy over free trade agreements and the benefits of market liberalisation. The 1994 North American Free Trade Agreement comes under a barrage of criticism from migration activists, who believe it has hastened the decline of small and medium-sized agriculture in Mexico that began with the Green Revolution of the 1940s and 1950s. Nafta has pushed campesinos off their land into the cities and forced millions to look for a new life in the US. The battleground is maize. Nafta has spewed subsidised US maize into Mexico, and hammered the price of local maize through the floor. Large, mechanised, low-labour agribusiness has survived but medium-sized farms have laid off their workers, often peasants supplementing subsistence farming with a daily wage. Alternative jobs in manufacturing for which these destitute people were meant to raise a glass have not materialised. In terms of numbers, migration into the US is now comparable to the exodus towards the cities inside Mexico itself. By the late 1990s, more than a million people a year were apprehended trying to cross into the US from Mexico without authorisation – a 40 per cent increase on 1994, when Nafta took effect and Mexico devalued the peso.

A feature of this liberal market emigration to the US is the rising number of indigenous people, the custodians of subsistence farming in southern Mexico, who appear to be crossing. Figures are hard to come by, but one sign of the flight from ruin is the presence in the US of Mexicans who barely speak Spanish. (At the Mexican Consulate in Tucson there are speakers of indigenous languages on call.) Native American groups are firmly opposed to the state immigration laws. The Navajo Nation Council spoke against SB1070 in 2010 and when Senator Pearce unveiled his new raft of bills in committee in 2011, Albert Hale, a former state senator and president of the Navajo Nation, was quick to observe that his people 'understand immigration from a different perspective': 'We have been subjected to undocumented immigration since day one, since 1492.' The Tohono O'odham, a native Indian people whose 4,500 square miles of desert reservation extend to the frontier, also opposed SB1070 on civil and human rights grounds, suspecting it would add racial profiling to their list of woes. The O'odham have never been reconciled to an international frontier that cuts their traditional lands in two. Now they argue that the recent security fixation has funnelled illegal activity their way from Mexico, ravaged the local ecology and seen Homeland Security building over their archaeological sites. Very many undocumented migrants cross via the reservation. Indeed this is where the red dots on the deaths map are mostly thickly clustered. Business in human and drug smuggling is brisk, some of it involving younger O'odham themselves. At the same time it is much harder now for O'odham living in Mexico to cross over and visit relatives, or for those living north of the border to reach sacred sites to the south. As aboriginal voices grow louder, they inject a powerful ingredient into the immigration debate: a sense of the *longue durée*, shared by all minorities who know they must wait it out. Slowly but surely the argument in Arizona is taking on the character of a New World dispute about who was here first.

Seen from this perspective, every lawmaker in the state capitol is a parvenu, and the main building itself, which was completed in 1901, has an air of callow officiousness. The point Reza and his fellow militants are making by performing ancestral rites on the lawns is clear enough: the historic annexations of Mexican land, the invention of Arizona, the founding of the state legislature, the creation of an international border and then of the category 'illegal' for people crossing it without papers: none of this is authoritative or venerable in their eyes (Latinos are fond of saying that they didn't cross the border, it crossed them). It is all much too recent and depends, in the last instance, on force rather than tradition.

Perhaps white people can be forgiven for imagining a reconquista by stealth and numbers, aided and abetted by an aboriginal rights renaissance. But if ethnic ideologies are in the air, it's largely in reaction to zealous border security and anti-immigration sentiment in the South-West, Arizona especially. Notwithstanding denials from Pearce and Brewer this sentiment, too, has a nativist undertone, which echoes loudly in the mannered style of law enforcement and incarceration. The sheriff of Maricopa County, Joe Arpaio, an influential eccentric obsessed by border issues (even though Maricopa does not extend to the border), is famous for forcing inmates in his jails to wear pink underwear, introducing pink handcuffs and making his detention facilities as humiliating as possible – Angélica described the food in one of Arpaio's jails as 'dog vomit'. A deportee I met in Mexico recalled several grim days in a county cell with no beds and a floor with raised joists at narrow intervals, making it impossible to lie down. Arpaio has also reintroduced chain gangs and set up an open-air tent city in Phoenix for detainees, apparently at Pearce's suggestion, to mini-mise detention costs. To his anti-migrant following this may well seem bracing and colourful but Arpaio has run up against the federal courts for violating prisoners' rights and for 'unconsti-tutional' searches. In a devastating profile for the *New Yorker* in 2009, William Finnegan showed that whatever the sheriff had spared the taxpayer by serving inedible food to inmates, it was nothing beside the millions demanded by the courts as compensa-tion for violent deaths in his custody.

Pearce was once chief deputy sheriff under Arpaio. They have since fallen out, but they still share a propensity to see border security and immigration in terms of America's epic national struggles against al-Qaida, for control of the Middle East and the pacification of Afghanistan. Pearce told me 'the greatest threat to homeland security' was the border and went on to say that 'four of the five conspirators' in the 9/11 hijackings had been stopped by law enforcement in the US and were 'in violation of immigra-tion laws'. In 2003, when Arpaio's prisoners, many of whom were undocumented migrants, complained of the soaring summer tem-peratures in his tent city, he reminded them that it was '120 degrees in Iraq, and the soldiers are living in tents and they didn't commit any crimes, so shut your mouths.' It's this readiness to envisage the same war on different fronts that has turned Arizona into a militarised desert principality: the adversary is hard to see, though drones and helicopter crews monitor the border, while the terrain itself is strewn with roadblocks, barriers, walls, fences, detach-ments of armed personnel, armoured vehicles, sniffer dogs and vigilantes.

I nearly forgot to add prisons. In December 2009, while Pearce was putting together support for SB1070, he made a presentation in Washington DC at a meeting of the American Legislative Exchange Council (ALEC). ALEC is an influence forum, where state politicians and corporate businessmen mull things over to their mutual advantage. The ALEC taskforce event at which Pearce sketched out his vision of SB1070 was attended by delegates from the Corrections Corporation of America, which runs more than sixty federal, state and city jails in the country. CCA liked Pearce's mission statement and proposed to help him draft his bill: migrant detention looked like the next big expansion for the company. The bill went on to win thirty-six sponsors in the Arizona statehouse and, according to an investigation by National Public Radio, thirty received donations from companies specialising in 'outsourced correctional services', including MTC, 'a leader in the management and operation of private correctional facilities', and the Geo Group (Geo UK runs Harmondsworth, the largest immigration detention centre in Europe). CCA was also a donor. Arizona has, *inter alia*, ten state penitentiaries, five federal prisons, five ICE detention centres for immigration offences, and eight county jails in Maricopa County alone.

It is hard to say how many people are under lock and key at any one time, but ICE currently has room for about 4,000 offenders and, pending massive expansion, it rents inmate space in local jails. A new county jail conveniently situated in Nogales can hold 370 inmates and takes federal detainees, almost all undocumented migrants, at a charge to the US government of $65 per inmate per night. There are 40,000 prisoners in the state's own penitentiaries. The law may be the bottom line for Pearce, but he needs help from the private sector. The detention industry, by happy coincidence, depends on law enforcement as the unique market for its expertise, and is the perfect partner for Pearce. Here, the analogy with distant wars holds up: similar relationships were forged in Iraq between the US government and companies like Halliburton or KBR, which made a tidy profit out of the invasion.

The difficulty for Pearce and his followers, and for Governor Brewer, is to convince opponents in the rest of the country that they are not racists, even though their legislation splits the community in Arizona along racial lines; or white supremacists, even though they have extremist ethnic supporters. The tide has run in their favour. They have come up against the federal courts but, more important, they have sounded a note of defiance to federal government: if it cannot enforce its immigration policy, it should mind its manners when states take matters into their own hands. This approach has served the politicians well, even though their complaints about Washington's indifference are largely posturing: Arizona is a net beneficiary of federal largesse, propped up by Obama's 2009 recovery programme to the tune of half the state's annual budget. The Obama administration has, in addition, put billions of dollars into border security, detention and deportation, some of it going direct to border states, including Arizona, for rental prison space.

Brewer and Pearce have gambled on SB1070 becoming a contagious piece of legislation and this, too, has paid off. By the end of 2010 at least sixteen state legislatures had introduced similar bills. Laws in Georgia have been countered by federal injunction but Arizona has ceded first place for 'rogue state' to Alabama, where an even more drastic version of SB1070 was upheld, on key points, by the federal courts in the autumn of 2011. The Obama administration has gone to appeal, but the bleak intransigence of Arizona's lawmakers is already a model for conservatives across the country.

More encouraging still, for Brewer and Pearce, is the unmistakable convergence between Arizona's rawhide approach and the humming policy machinery in Washington. Take Homeland Security's Secure Communities programme, road-tested under Bush and implemented by Obama. The S-Comm approach is very close to that of SB1070: overlapping state and federal law enforcement, fingerprint-sharing between the two – the 'integrated biometric database' – and the escalation of parking violations into evictions. It is essentially a deportation mechanism, which attempts with mixed success to target undocumented migrants involved in serious crime. In the first five months of 2011, around

30,000 people were deported under S-Comm, some 25 per cent charged with serious crimes and 32 per cent with immigration violations only.

The Obama administration is in a mess over S-Comm. Illinois, New York and Massachusetts are seeking to withdraw, arguing that the programme undermines trust between local police and immigrant communities, but the administration insisted in 2011 that no state could opt out. At the same time Homeland Security put 300,000 planned deportations – of unauthorised migrants, already detained, but with no criminal record – on hold, as a result of intense pressure from Hispanic communities. Then in June 2012, Obama announced from the Rose Garden that unauthorised migrants who had arrived before the age of sixteen, were under thirty, had been in the US continuously for a minimum of five years and had no criminal record would not be pursued or deported on account of their status. It was the first step on the path to citizenship for roughly 800,000 young people, mostly Latinos. With one well-timed executive order the president had rallied Hispanic leaders for the November election, complicated Romney's campaign strategy, and found favour with activists and immigrants across the country.

Obama's position has not been easy to read. At times he has seemed to be dancing to two tunes, as the band in Arizona plays for all it's worth. At others the music sounds like variations on a single theme. He has presided, after all, over roughly a million deportations since the beginning of 2009, a greater number than Bush in any comparable period and perhaps a record for any US president: no one knows for sure how many Mexicans were thrown out during Operation Wetback. One million is yet another figure to keep in mind when the time comes to look back on the Obama legacy.

Pearce's astonishing tenure came under serious attack in Arizona at the end of 2011, when a recall voting procedure based on a citizens' petition succeeded in forcing him from office before his term was up. It was a shock for the senator and a moment of hard-won satisfaction for his opponents, but by 2012 he was running for re-election. After the Supreme Court decision on SB1070 in the summer, he was in high spirits. He and his followers understand that in the long term the demography will turn against ethnic ultra-conservatism, but the short term has been compelling. Pearce always accused his political opponents of seeking 'cheap votes' as well as 'cheap labour', yet there was something cheap, too, about his own insistence on the threat of lawless brown people at a time when figures for illegal entry were plummeting. Had he factored in the people who never made it across the desert? Were fresh cohorts of spectral Mexicans gliding through the cactus in terrifying numbers, whispering to the living who trudged beside them? In any case, Pearce's vision worked with the voters of Arizona, where many Latinos who might have fought back are not on the electoral register, while 58 per cent of the state's population is white non-Hispanic. Since 2008, Arizona has risen to second place in the list of states with the most poverty – Mississippi is still ahead – but it remains a retirement haven for elderly, prosperous whites who vote with their putters. White nativism may not have time on its side, but it's had money and power to be going on with.

Not long after Senator Pearce had given me the time of day, I went back into Mexico and met up with Father Pete, a Jesuit priest from Douglas, AZ, who was on a visit to a feeding centre for deportees. There were scores of newly deported and a handful of hangers-on, eating at long tables in a breeze-block building with a kitchen to the side. Grace was said before beans and tortillas. A plausible ne'er-do-well, in his forties, told me he'd been raised as a child in California, lived in the US ever since, and been deported a few days earlier. He'd been arrested on suspicion of a minor felony and his papers were out of order. His name was Moisés. He was trying to get back to the US, but the Red Sea wouldn't part for him. He saw it clearly now, he was a fugitive. Yet the real disaster, he went on, was that he'd been blissfully unaware of the fact for years. He was broke, clean-shaven and well turned out, even though, like many deportees who fetched up for a plate of food that afternoon, he was sleeping rough – in a nearby cemetery. Others had crossed once, twice, several times, and been turfed back over the border. A Guatemalan man and his wife were peeling potatoes for the next day's wave of deportees. We struck up a conversation and they rehearsed their harrowing journey through Mexico, a long story, and before it was done, Father Pete had tapped me on the shoulder: it was dusk and time to head back to the United States. The husband apologised. It turned out he'd only taken us as far as his first attempt at the border, a year or more ago. On that occasion, they'd been caught, jailed and flown back to Guatemala City by the federal authorities. So where were we now? I asked in haste. They had just failed on their second bid, two days earlier, but at least they weren't back at square one. They aimed to try again within the month. The man was small and rugged; in Guatemala City he'd worked in construction. His wife was smaller still and about as rugged as it gets. The Sonoran Desert, and arrest and detention in the US, were nothing beside the dangers they'd faced on their first trip through Mexico. Father Pete gave them his high pastoral fives and the couple went back to their work.

The consensus is that about eleven million undocumented migrants are living in the US. Bear Stearns took a punt, a few years before its demise, and put the figure at twenty million: somewhere, in any case, between 3 and 7 per cent of the population. One answer to this is an amnesty package, which would legalise their presence and offer them the possibility of citizenship later on. Reagan signed an amnesty bill in 1986, when four to six million people were living unlawfully in the US, many from Central America, whose asylum claims would have contradicted Washington's stated objectives in the region. Since then, the figure has risen again and a new act is overdue, yet in recent years four Comprehensive Immigration Reform bills have been introduced and failed, despite powerful backing (John McCain, Bush Jr, Edward Kennedy). During his presidential campaign, Obama spoke in favour of reform – he spoke in favour of many things – but went on to become a border security politician by default until his dramatic concession to Hispanic voters in 2012.

The pressures of inward migration to wealthy parts of the developed world since the 1970s suggest that amnesty programmes, introduced from time to time, or even triggered when figures rise beyond an agreed level, are a sensible way to manage liberal societies with high numbers of undocumented migrants. No responsible state wants unentitled people hidden in the creases of the wider social fabric. The legislation that has stalled in Congress since 2005 would have made what happened to Oscar and Ricardo, the two young men in Nogales, impossible. It would have raised tax revenues. It might well have reduced the jet-black areas of the grey economy, where undocumented migrants find themselves trafficked into lives of semi-slavery. It might also have allowed wages among the poorest paid US citizens – invariably African-American – to hold up better than they have. These would be real achievements and the idea of comprehensive immigration reform has not gone away. There are proposals for a new bill and powerful voices in its favour, including that of Michael Bloomberg's Partnership for a New American Economy – a partnership with Rupert Murdoch, among others.

Almost every high-profile proponent of amnesty, including Bloomberg and Murdoch, endorses a fortress approach to illegal immigration (the phrase is normally 'secure our borders'). Hardliners on the right don't believe what they're being told: to them it is a hollow quid pro quo from people whose real intention is to create millions of new Americans. Pearce described it as 'hypocrisy', though no partner for a new American economy loses sleep over poverty in Latin America. Bloomberg et al want to 'attract and keep the best, the brightest and the hardest working': they acknowledge a need for low-wage service personnel and hardy seasonal labour, in the Bracero tradition – amnesty offers the prospect of a large pool of legal labour – but the emphasis still falls on skilled, well-educated migrants. That leaves many rural poor, dispersed by their government's economic programmes and battered by free trade agreements, waiting on the wrong side of the threshold, along with growing numbers of unemployed in cities near the border: in Ciudad Juárez, once a Nafta showcase, now ravaged by guns and drugs, unemployment is running at around 20 per cent.

The advantages of market liberalisation have been slow to migrate away from wealthier countries, while the battered ideal of the free market, like the battered ideal of Communism, has brought ruin on smallholders, as collectivisation did, and offered little in return. It continues to promise Mexicans everything if only they would renew their faith in the doctrine. In Mexico, where the World Bank estimates that more than 40 per cent of the population live in poverty, people have been clinging on since the convulsive market reforms of the 1980s. In the orthodox model, goods, services and capital must circulate freely, while economic justice remains a sovereign affair, subject, just as human beings are, to the law of the frontier. This anomaly, framed by border security, drives millions of Latinos north to redress it themselves, and accounts for the fact that the migrant remittance, at roughly $25 billion a year, is now Mexico's second highest source of external income. Depriving lower wage-earners of the opportunity to send money back to their families at home compounds their poverty and ensures continued pressure on the border.

Migration out of Mexico may well become the war that Homeland Security has anticipated. The phenomenology of the US/Mexico frontier is martial: a vast, straggling set of defences, edified at extraordinary cost, where America's sense that it is under siege can be properly enacted. To believe in this story, you have to imagine that the miserable encampment in Nogales where I found Oscar and Ricardo is really the tent of Achilles. But if you do, you must also accept that the Trojans have something they should negotiate. Whites in Arizona don't: in their parochial version of the tale, tens of thousands of undocumented Mexicans are infiltrating every year into territory that is too close for comfort to Mexico. And if they peer over the edge of the border debate, at an epic in which human movement is not just the pursuit of a better life but a competitive struggle for food, energy and water, their worries seem doubly justified. Many white nativist websites assert, correctly, that population increase in Arizona will be hard to sustain; none admits that the frontier is an artificial line across interlocking eco-systems, under pressure from top-heavy consumer lifestyles to the north and a congestion of poverty in the south. The result is a twi-light world of flight, seclusion and incarceration, with Hispanics eager to leave the state for other parts of the US. Those who remain lapse into self-employment lite, staying at home when they can, reluctant even to pick up a set of car keys. The less fortu-nate are hauled into custody, to service the rituals of authority and humiliation, which Sheriff Arpaio means to perfect by putting his prisoners to work on the building of more prison space for more prisoners, the great majority undocumented migrants.

Most weekdays you can see the same rituals performed in the federal court house in Tucson, as new detainees apprehended near the border, anything from fifty upwards at a single hearing, are sen-tenced under a programme that whisks them through a shorthand criminal procedure and off to deportation, or a jail term ending in deportation. Enthusiasts claim that Operation Streamline is bring-ing down the number of unauthorised crossings. Numbers happen to be falling, but Streamline is only one of several factors in play. The price of this courtroom spectacle is exorbitant. Where else in the world does a court resound with the noise of rattling chains, as prisoners, shackled at the feet and handcuffed, sit in rows – women in one area, men in another – and stir from time to time, waiting to be called before the bench in groups of seven, where they make their way like hobbled animals, have their names read to them, are asked if they understand their rights, and then enter a guilty plea? Sentences are handed down at breakneck speed, some as low as thirty days, others as high as 180, all followed by deportation. As one batch nods a cursory thanks to their lawyers, and US marshals lead them away, another seven shuffle forward to the bench. Many still have the dust of a failed crossing on their clothes. They might be prisoners taken on the field of battle.

'It's not pretty, is it?' the judge asked when we met a few minutes after one such hearing. He reckoned that in his court, Streamline costs $50,000 a week in attorneys' fees alone. When he added

Streamline and the other fast-track judicial procedures together, the best outcome he could see was about 8,000 deportations a month. 'Ask yourself if that makes a difference,' he said, pulling the wrapper from a nicotine substitute. Anyone can research the correct answer. There are already 500,000 undocumented Hispanic residents in Arizona alone. In 2010, along the length of the frontier with Mexico, Border Patrol caught more than 400,000 people trying to enter without authorisation. Perhaps its three-for-one estimate is an exaggeration, but we can safely assume that a good many people slipped across a frontier which has never articulated north and south to the satisfaction of either party. Why should it do so now? Unfair, leaky immigration systems, the kind we have learned to live with, express this contradiction even as they struggle to manage it. But what is it that's expressed by the radical wish to exclude, imprison and deport? And what kind of management is that?

5

He arrived in Basra and went to the shop belonging to the fat man whose job was smuggling people into Kuwait. He stood before him, bearing on his shoulders all the humiliation and hope that an old man can carry. And there was a blanket of echoing silence after the fat proprietor of the office had repeated:

'It's a difficult journey, I tell you. It will cost you fifteen dinars.'

'And you can guarantee that we shall arrive safely?'

'Of course you will arrive safely. But you will have to suffer a little discomfort. You know, we are in August now. The heat is intense and the desert has no shade. But you will arrive.'

Ghassan Kanafani, *Men in the Sun*

In Western Europe – the western Mediterranean particularly – it is impossible to follow asylum seekers without running across large numbers of 'economic migrants' who also enter illegally, mostly from Albania and North and sub-Saharan Africa. Unlike most of the world's migrants, they are not well-to-do. Many are poor; others who may look poor are simply run ragged, drained by the distances they've covered, including an arduous desert crossing: the Sonora desert and the Sahara impose high costs for anyone who takes a chance.

The people I'd seen ferried from an abandoned hulk off the coast of southern Italy in 1998 were typical: the fatigue, and the sense of relief, were palpable. Then there was the brusque 'Up, up' – a haunting summary of the thousands of miles that one migrant from Sierra Leone had put behind him. And the flip of the hand, which seemed to toss so many questions into the air. How do you make your way from Freetown to a dank little Italian port in winter, where the rain is sheeting down onto the concrete quays? Had he come across the Sahara? As a clandestine migrant from a country that was at war at the time, he might well have expected leave to remain on humanitarian grounds. But what if he had come from Niger or Mauritania or Nigeria? What if he had fled, not from direct, political persecution, but from a state of affairs so bad that it was intolerable, or even life-threatening, to stay?

The UN High Commissioner for Refugees publishes a hand-book advising on procedures and criteria for determining refugee status. In the chapter dealing with 'Inclusion Clauses', the advice is as follows: 'The distinction between an economic migrant and a refugee is sometimes blurred ... Where economic measures destroy the economic existence of a particular section of the popu-lation ... the victims may, according to the circumstances, become refugees on leaving the country.' And then, sounding a more cau-tious note: 'Objections to general economic measures are not by themselves good reason for claiming refugee status.' The intention of this passage is to circumscribe and reinforce the right of asylum by ruling out the possibility of a claim on grounds of poverty alone. But it also concedes that poverty may be a form of torment – and in broader terms, that it may often wait on persecution. The care that is taken to distinguish refugees from other, disadvantaged migrants is perfectly proper. In the meantime, there is plenty of evidence to suggest that those who try to enter the rich world by stealth in search of a livelihood are not much better off than refugees. Often they are worse off.

In the late 1990s, when the number of illegal migrants leapt in Italy, the newspapers were full of editorials about the resulting 'social and ethnic tensions'. But 'social' tension within Italy and other Western European states has more to do with the geo-economic strain between the rich world and the poor world – and 'ethnic' tension is merely a variation on that theme. Forty or fifty years ago, Italians who arrived in a northern city like Milan from the south of the country were mistrusted in much the same way as North Africans, Albanians and Nigerians are now. They were the ethnic migrants of their day.

Until 1961, when the Fascist 'anti-urbanisation' law was repealed, tens, perhaps hundreds of thousands of 'undocumented' persons lived and worked illegally in the north of Italy. They were said to be noisy, or violent, or predisposed to crime, just as Albanians and Maghrebis are now. The difference is that by and large Italian migrants who headed north in the 1950s and 1960s found remunerative work in a highly industrialised environment. In most of the West, this sector has shrunk. Whatever their qualifications, many of the new migrants coming off the beaches of southern Italy depend in the settling-in period on piecemeal work or fragile havens in the informal sector colonised by their fellow nationals, where jobs are unpredictable and often underpaid. They also rely on the well-established economy of criminal or semi-criminal activity.

Clandestine migrants or foreigners residing in Italy without proper papers become involved in passport and ID scams and, in Milan especially, many work at the sharp end of drug dealing and the sex industry. There are jobs in the North, of the kind that Italian migrants would have found in the 1960s – a proportion of workers in the steel companies of the North-East are sub-Saharan Africans – but there are fewer of them now, and the alternatives for those migrants who are drawn into criminal activity are less obvious.

The connection between crime and clandestine migration, however, may not be a result of the change in Western economies. Since the years of vigorous South-North migration in Italy, or Commonwealth migration to Britain, the service sector in the West has expanded dramatically; it has also become a source of jobs for women and minorities. Migrant self-employment and the phenomenon known as 'ethnic small business', with its many vexations – including 'self-exploitation' and the exploitation of family members – are on the increase too. At the same time, a growing number of service providers and small businesses now operate in the shadow economies of wealthy countries, where employers are ignoring the law. When clandestine immigrants find themselves embroiled with illegality after their arrival in a rich country, it is often because of the nature of the work on offer and the fact that they may still be bound to the trafficking organisations that brought them in.

Many are themselves the object of criminal or unacceptable activity. In the Netherlands, for example, most aspects of prostitution are legal, but in Amsterdam in the mid-1990s, 75 per cent of the 'window girls' were non-nationals and of these, according to the Dutch police, 80 per cent were in the country illegally. The number of women arriving from the former Eastern bloc rose sharply in the early 1990s, as did the number of men suspected of trafficking. The central problem in all this has been the ownership of the women and the appropriation of their earnings. When a court in Brussels convicted nine members of a Nigerian prostitution network in 1997, it emerged that the recruits had been promised asylum in order to entice them out of West Africa. They could buy their freedom from the pimping circuits in Germany, Italy and Belgium for $25,000. Indenture and exploitation are the crimes here – and, you could argue, insatiable demand in the marketplace. The same is true of young males trafficked for sexual purposes: in this under-investigated world, a victim may be guilty of some minor misdemeanour – drug use, petty theft, the habits of radical urban homelessness – or a stigma may attach to him because he is gay, or sometimes transsexual, but he has committed none of the serious crimes with which he's associated by being trafficked. Like the female prostitute or the person of any colour, age or gender in bonded labour, or the child soldier in DR Congo, he can only be said to collude. There were 12.3 million adults and children in forced labour, bondage or involuntary prostitution in 2010, according to the US State Department.

The spread of information, and information technology, and the accessibility of international travel (cheaper airfares, rising numbers of passengers) put strains on restrictive immigration and perhaps, too, an onus on people to circumvent them. A satellite channel on the TV in a village café, a mobile phone in a refugee camp or, higher up the scale of prosperity, an email facility in an office that depends on an electricity generator, no longer seem odd: they were already platitudes before the millennium. It is possible to send and receive – in poorer countries, mostly to receive – in ways that have certainly foreshortened the distances between continents. But these seductive forms of abbreviation on which we congratulate ourselves are like tricks of perspective that make the horizon appear closer than it is. The real effect of digital and satellite communication is to pitch the world into a more advanced state of anomaly. A Bulgarian car worker and his Danish counterpart can purchase the same luxury item – a colour television, for instance – but the first will have to work for half a year to acquire what the second can afford after half a week on the job. Nowadays, however, the Bulgarian worker is constantly being reminded of the relative purchasing power of the Dane – and it is certain that he gives this discrepancy a good deal of thought. The father of a desperate family in Burkina Faso who decides, after three bad harvests in a row, to ride into town and negotiate a loan can watch a weight-loss commercial on CNN while he waits in the living room of a prestigious uncle. He is already too familiar with anomaly to take offence at what he sees: he will think of it as a form of empty magic rather than a taunt. But market capitalism is always taunting the poor, and it now has far more scope to do so than it had in the heyday of the postwar advertising moguls.

In the least developed countries, the message of globalisation is fairly constant: stay put at all costs; help is on its way. But when the remedy takes longer to work than the doctors anticipated, the urge to get up becomes harder to resist, because globalisation heightens the contradiction between promise, which is ever-extensive, and reality, which is much as it was. If salvation keeps failing to appear over the brow of the hill, it may be time to leave the plain. The poor begin to grasp that they should follow the money, since it has failed to seek them out. Some of them take the lesson to heart.

In 1990 the UN produced a finicky but useful improvement on GDP per capita as a measure of the quality of life in any given country. The Human Development Index takes account of adult literacy, life expectancy, income levels and the average number of years a child spends in school. The results are not so much profiles of countries as silhouettes, projected against a twilight of statistics. In the human development ratings compiled by the UN, the citizens of about ninety countries could be said to enjoy a good quality of life. The remainder are caught in the slough of middling to low. In the top ninety countries, which include Bolivia, Slovakia and Albania, there are no entries whatever from sub-Saharan Africa – not even South Africa, the jewel in the continent's crown.

There is also the sensitive barometer of comparative wealth known as the PPP (or 'purchasing power parity') index, a measure of the relative ability of the world's inhabitants to pay for goods and services, which we encountered in Chapter 3. It is derived by adjusting exchange rates to take account of cost-of-living differences, which are calculated, in turn, on the variable price of those goods and services across the globe. A rough hierarchy of national purchasing power can be obtained by running the per capita GDP of every country through the adjusted exchange rate. The result is expressed in a point system, with the US citizen scoring 100 points, the Luxembourgeois 116.1 and, at the *bas-fonds* of the index, the farmer in Myanmar fewer than 5. Of the twenty-five entries at the bottom of the GDP (PPP) per capita list, twenty-three are sub-Saharan. In terms of the Human Development Index and PPP, globalisation in Africa is a busted flush.

Why, then, are there so few sub-Saharan hands rattling the portcullis? By comparison with Asia and Eastern Europe, Africa is a modest source of legal and clandestine migration to the rich world, despite the strength of old colonial ties to several EU countries. It is thought that fewer than five million sub-Saharan Africans live outside their region, although in the EU alone, there are around twenty-two million third-country immigrants in total. Part of the reason is the lure of South Africa, which drew on a large pool of migratory labour from neighbouring states under apartheid and remains a magnet for continental expatriates, who now come from further afield, including Nigeria and DR Congo. Most sub-Saharans who leave their region aim for the Maghreb: Libya, with its pan-African pretensions, encouraged this trend in the 1990s and has since sent many migrants on into other Maghreb countries. The numbers of sub-Saharans attempting passage from North Africa to Europe by sea are on the rise, but they remain in the tens of thousands.

The African case raises one of the great conundrums facing governments that want to keep out migrants from poorer countries, for it suggests that high levels of immiseration such as Africa has endured since the 1970s are not the decisive cause of migration to the rich world. It is true that many clandestine migrants are driven by poverty, but there are also many whose levels of prosperity and whose quality of life are the very factors that enable them to leave. Wealthy states – EU member states, for instance – who hope to discourage migration from very poor parts of the world by a cautious transfer of resources (more advantageous bilateral trade deals, deeper debt relief and so on) should not be downcast if they discover, after a few years, that these initiatives have failed to keep the adventurous few from leaving their target countries. For a country that did indeed show an increase in GDP, adult literacy and life expectancy – a general improvement all round – would be likely to produce even more aspiring migrants than a country trying to cope with live burial at the bottom of the world economy.

For thirty years or more, Mexico was the most obvious case of the rapid growth/high sender economy, even though numbers have dipped sharply since 2008. But the broad thrust of modern migration, away from rural areas to sprawling conurbations, holds true for almost any developing country. When an agricultural revolution tears through the patterns of subsistence farming, the dispossessed are not the only people driven to the city. The beneficiaries of surplus make their way there too, buying into education and new skills: the potential for mobility, unleashed in the villages, carries well beyond the national capital.

The problem for rich nations aiming at minimal immigration from poorer countries is obvious: in attempting to discourage migration by enriching source countries, they can never rule out the possibility that they are stimulating the very phenomenon they wished to depress. In the past, a government's immigration policy amounted to a yes or a no, according to its needs and wishes, and the ability to enforce its word at its frontiers. Nowadays, it involves byzantine projections that take into account the likely effect, in terms of migratory pressure, of one region being enriched or another impoverished, and complex bilateral negotiations with source countries over migrant quotas. All the while, governments strenuously resist the conclusion about the free movement of people that they reached with equanimity about the free movement of capital: that it may be an expensive waste of time to try to fend it off.

Nobody is sure what a liberalisation of human movement would look like, any more than we could be certain in the 1980s what the deregulation of world markets would entail. Would the consequences of human beings moving around more freely than they do now turn out to be just as momentous? And would the old mechanisms of power persist in some form that left the rich world with a controlling interest in who went where (or who didn't), much as the corporate establishments of the old order were able to safeguard their ascendancy during and after deregulation?

The answers to these questions are deferred for as long as developed countries remain wedded to restrictive immigration. If they could conceive of a world in which movement was freer than it is, they might find it easier to resolve some of the more pressing problems that accompany restriction on movement now. The most obvious of these is that it becomes costlier and more of a nuisance to maintain when even a handful of aspiring migrants in poorer countries – whether they are in the process of becoming richer or not – cease to respect the borders of wealthier ones. Another is that restriction tends to encourage migrants who want real freedom of movement – which is to say, the legal right to enter and leave at their leisure – to opt for settlement or some form of long-term residency. To enter a country with a strict immigration policy, often after a good deal of paperwork and a large financial outlay, is to feel a nagging fear that next time it could all be harder; that access, which in a perfect world would be available on demand, could be cut off at any time by a surge of anti-immigration feeling or a new round of restrictive legislation.

Only those who are persecuted or cut to the quick by poverty want to uproot permanently and fight for their place in a society where they are unwelcome. Others would sooner have the right to come and go. Europe is far from establishing any such right. In its absence, immigrants arriving from poorer countries in the last fifty years have decided, after due consideration, that the best course of action is to dig in.

It is one thing for an immigrant to take up the burden of exile for the duration of his working life and another for an entrepreneur to fly in and fly out as he pleases; to buy goods and ship them home, install them or sell them on, and build up a business that requires more frequent visits to the rich world, more substantial purchases. Restrictive immigration tends to deny the short-term visitor the ability to spend directly in Europe. The West prefers foreign consumers to purchase at one remove, normally through the costly mediation of Western agents and middlemen: prudence is the loyal servant of seclusion.

In *A Seventh Man* (1975), John Berger described the vicissitudes of clandestine migration from Portugal through Spain into France. Smugglers charged $350 per person, about a year's earnings for a peasant farmer when migration from Portugal was still illegal. Often, they cheated their clients by abandoning them in the mountains across the Spanish frontier. The migrants devised a system to guard against this:

> Before leaving they had their photographs taken. They tore the photograph in half, giving one half to their 'guide' and keeping the other for themselves. When they reached France they sent

half of the photograph back to their family in Portugal to show
that they had been safely escorted across the frontiers; the 'guide'
came to the family with his half of the photograph to prove that
it was he who had escorted them, and it was only then that the
family paid the $350.

There are similar arrangements now. Families in China pay the
agents' fees in instalments. They keep to the schedule only when
a clandestine émigré has confirmed his safe arrival in Britain,
where he, too, can make a contribution – the cost in 2000 was in
the region of £15,000 and rising – but many forms of servitude and
exploitation are involved. Failure to pay can lead to the victimisa-
tion or disappearance of the migrant. What Berger's account of
Portuguese clandestines has in common with stories today is the
importance, to those who remain behind, of sending out a relative
who can shore up the family economy with earnings and establish a
base, of which other family members may one day take advantage.

Migrants from Africa, the Middle East and the remains of the
Eastern bloc are foragers, an advance guard, illustrious adventur-
ers – potential earners above all. They also act as intermediaries
between two worlds. In the North, by their example, they vouch
for the rigorous nineteenth-century logic of 'amelioration' and, in
setting their hands to anything, offer a moral lesson in endurance
and versatility. They find a rapt audience – captive, in fact – in
their countries of origin, whom they regale with tales of sumptu-
ous indulgence and untold risk. But there are also long interludes
of realism. By reporting back, or visiting, or returning for good
after five, ten, fifteen years, migrants reinforce the scepticism of
sedentary communities about the footling self-portraiture that
the rich world disseminates on the Internet and satellite TV. In
all this, it is not a picture of themselves that migrants complete by
supplying the missing part, but a picture of the world beyond the
village or the township. They can paraphrase, gloss and interpret
the ramblings of the prosperous democracies and sound a warning
that the land of riches may be bleak and unforgiving, despite its
advantages. As more migrants arrive in Western Europe, the

demystification of the rich world gains ground. Those who enter now have fewer illusions than their predecessors, who would often rather they did not follow in their footsteps. Their successors will have fewer still, but they will keep wanting to come.

Sustaining the remittance, rolling access to foreign income across two generations, extending it, seeing it through – these are powerful motives for migrants, even though they are under suspicion in places where they can earn a living. In the early 1990s, when the IMF reviewed the global value of remittances, it estimated that migrants had transferred $65 billion out of their host countries in 1989; this figure exceeded by about $20 billion all official development assistance from donor states to qualifying countries in the same year. By 2010 international migrants were remitting $440 billion per annum, according to IMF research, while official development assistance remained below $150 billion. For families in a country like Tunisia, to which workers abroad now remit nearly $2 billion a year, or Haiti – in the region of $1.7 billion – earners posted overseas for long periods are crucial.

If freedom of movement is a 'human right', as some argue, there must also be a case for the rights of communities to oppose what they do not want, including immigration. A community that successfully defeats a proposal for a local nuclear reactor is safer, by a margin, if it is built three hundred miles away instead. That is some kind of victory. Similarly, if it deflects a prospective motorway or defeats a plan to bus in children from other neighbourhoods to its schools, it is ensuring that things go on as they did. Victory here, too. The adverse effect on other communities will, of course, have negative repercussions on the one whose strength of feeling spared it the brunt of the difficulty: no parish is an island. But restricting immigration may not even amount to a parochial victory.

The reason for this is connected with population growth and the tendency of poorer people to invest in kind – that is to say, in even greater numbers of poorer people, via the low-outlay strategy of having children. The restriction of migration to the rich world not only slows up the transfer of resources from rich to poor, and hampers the stewardship of local resources in poorer countries: it encourages higher rates of population growth in the world as a whole. With a net global population increase of eighty million people a year between now and 2040, this is not a welcome situation, even for communities whose own populations are in decline. In one account, the poor will begin to congregate at the gates in far higher numbers than they do already.

This possibility is set out in *The Lugano Report* (1999), a serio-comic investigation by Susan George, in which she imagines the findings of a panel of experts, commissioned by wealthy 'masters of the universe' to examine how best to keep global capitalism 'ticking over' to their advantage. The panel is dismayed by high population growth in poorer countries and the sluggish pace of wealth transfers from North to South. It foresees a huge increase in migratory pressure on the rich world. Migrant groups 'which Northern states already find difficult to assimilate into their mainstream, represent a mere fraction of those who will seek to migrate in future, as recurrent and widespread political economic and ecological breakdowns strike their own societies'.

The alarmist tone is deliberate – designed to point up the worst fears of wealthy states. But we know that at present only a very small proportion of the world's population migrate between continents: the remainder are immobile, listless even. By contrast, the panel's conclusions about the stress to which rising numbers of people subject the environment, based on projections of a world population increase from six billion at the millennium to anything between eight and twelve billion by 2050, are depressingly familiar: 'mass deforestation, species habitat destruction, mushrooming, unliveable and polluted cities, lakes and seas dead from industrial and human wastes; all constantly intensified by ever-growing multitudes', the 'substance of the earth … consumed' – and so on.

This throws a darker, less fantastic shadow over Europe's idyll of seclusion. We know for a fact that increasing numbers of displaced people in poorer countries are environmental refugees – people who are forced to abandon their homes because of a metropolitan hunger for fossil fuels, minerals, hardwoods, water and red meat.

We also know that the world's poorer communities become more numerous until their living standards improve, along with the spread of education and wider margins of choice, particularly for women of child-bearing age. Such improvements may raise their contribution to atmospheric pollution, global warming and every other item on the list of devastation – but no serious environmentalist advocates the villain's default option, of ensuring that even if the poor increase their numbers, they remain too abject to consume and pollute with the ferocity of a country like the US. Those who believe that the most urgent business now is the race against environmental depletion might reflect on liberal immigration as a way to win it. To insulate the rich world against the poor migrant is simply to fail at one of the early hurdles – improvement in living standards in underdeveloped countries – and sooner or later to take the consequences. For the future of the Alpine valley, whatever its collective sensibilities and however keen its antipathy towards people of another colour or culture, the absence of non-Europeans in the cheerful micro-ecology of '*l'espace européen*' has far more alarming implications than their presence.

The impending shortage of young people in a marketplace that has aimed to capture and consume the young by fattening them up into gainful consumers is also a cause for concern. Most population projections for Western Europe forecast rising numbers of elderly and falling numbers of young people – a witch's cage without Hansel and Gretel. This may account for the extremes of anger and dismay with which the West greets the arrival of 'unaccompanied minors': children from a poor or dangerous country who set out under their own steam for a richer, more stable destination, or who are sent by worried relatives and dumped, normally without any adult to ensure their safe arrival.

In these powerful symbolic figures the rich world discerns the hazy demographic issues at the back of migration and begins to understand that youth and age are no longer about time, so much as space. Life expectancy in many parts of the developing world is on the increase; in others, it will remain low. But in Europe, since

1945, old age has become one of the certainties of youth. When a ten-year-old girl from Togo is hoisted over the border fence of a Mediterranean outpost of Spanish Africa and left for police patrols to find, when half a dozen Ethiopian children are discovered huddling somewhere in Arrivals at Heathrow Airport, or the miraculous survivor of a flight in the undercarriage of an Air Afrique carrier from Senegal claims asylum in France, an extraordinary encounter takes place between a world defined largely by an excess of young people and another by a deficit.

In its distress at the arrival of unaccompanied minors, the rich world looks busily beyond them in search of someone to blame: the people who put them up to it – parents or relatives, traffickers or smugglers acting on their behalf, ruthless opportunists with no notion of decency. The real transgressors, however, are the uninvited children themselves, crossing the forbidden boundary between two worlds that resemble enchanted domains in a myth of primal sundering. In the first, there is only eternal youth, endlessly extinguished and replaced; here the young seem to have swallowed up the aged. In the second, crowds of mature adults and elderly extend the limits of longevity, deferring the moment of death, unwilling to cross the threshold but unable to return and regenerate the landscape over which they hastened; here the old have begun to devour the young. The youthful intruder in the province of age is a reminder that the child is no longer father to the man. In one place, the child reproduces himself on a treadmill of infirmity and social upheaval; in another, the father reproduces himself in the tender embrace of evolving medical technology.

That globalisation has failed to coax or bully these two worlds into closer relation was the drift of a letter found in the landing gear of an Airbus that flew out of Guinea-Conakry in the summer of 1999. It was recovered in Brussels from the wheel enclosure under the starboard wing of the aircraft, along with the remains of two young Africans who had stowed away in the hope of migrating to Europe. In the letter, addressed to 'Messrs the members and leaders of Europe', the two boys, Yaguine Koita and Fodé

Tounkara, explained what had led them to make a bid for the rich world: they were fugitives from the misfortune of happening to be African. The letter talks mostly of Africa and Africans – the words occur nine or ten times, the name of their own country only twice. Perhaps they made the astute assumption that no one in Europe would know where Guinea was. Or perhaps they felt strongly that their impasse in the shanties of Conakry was shared by millions of sub-Saharans. In their last will and testament, the two boys appeal to Europe's 'sense of solidarity and kindness … Help us, we suffer too much in Africa, help us.' They nominated 'war, sickness, food' as the great 'problems' of Africa and lamented the state of African schools. The overriding motive for their departure, they claimed, was to risk everything for an education. Here too, perhaps they gambled cynically, against long odds, that their sentimental appeal to the right to education would move European hearts and minds. 'We want to study and we ask you to help us to study to be like you in Africa.' They hid in the allotments at the near end of the airport runway and waited while a Sabena carrier taxied towards them. As it swung around to line up for take-off, they leapt the airport fence, sprinted under the howling turbines and clambered into the undercarriage. It is unusual to survive for very long at minus forty or fifty centigrade. Koita and Tounkara died like polar explorers in some terrifying ether ice field.

In Belgium, life expectancy is roughly double that of Guinea, while confidence in longevity is now normal in the West and China; it is a sign that we can still venerate old age while modelling youth as a market. In the US the so-called sandwich generation is growing: one in eight people between the ages of forty and sixty is bringing up a child and looking after an elderly relative at the same time. In China the one-child policy has become the 'four-parent policy': the absence of pensions outside the government sector and a few big companies means that couples must now support two sets of parents as well as a child, in an arrangement often referred to as 4:2:1. In Australia, Europe and North America, not only is the natural increase in population slowing up, but the foreign share of total births – always higher, proportionately, than the ratio of foreign to indigenous inhabitants – is failing to compensate. In wealthy countries, neither immigration nor higher numbers of births among naturalised foreigners or non-nationals can make up for the imminent shortage of young people.

Older people, we are told, will no longer be able to live in the manner to which they are accustomed. 'Very high volumes of migration would be needed,' the OECD declared in 1998, 'to change the trend in ageing populations' in prosperous countries. The analogy might be a full basin of water with the tap running. Now remove the plug. The first gurgling sounds are audible a little later, when the prevailing ratio of citizens between the ages of fifteen and sixty-four to citizens aged sixty-five or over is no longer sustainable. In 2000 the UN Population Division sounded the alarm by suggesting that the decline of the EU's population could only be redressed by an intake of some forty-seven million migrants before 2050. To maintain the number of inhabitants of working age would require perhaps 1.6 million new migrants every year. In the US the figure is lower: about 1,300 migrants annually for every one million inhabitants, i.e. around a million. But 'replacement migration', or adjusting for an ageing population, is a notion fraught with difficulty, not least because of the high figures involved and their political implications. There is no evidence that it can reverse a greying trend, only that it can slow it up until, eventually, the same ageing demographic starts to affect sender countries in Eastern Europe, say, or Latin America.

In any case the rich world cannot draw migrant labour only from the very poorest countries with the youngest demographic – from Guinea, for example. It will find sources closer to home (the first big supplier of migrant labour to industrialised Germany in the 1950s was Italy; it was followed by Spain and Greece, Turkey, Morocco, Portugal, Tunisia and Yugoslavia). Prosperous nations also look to parts of the world with a modicum of social and economic infrastructure, or places in which they have become embroiled through trade and the prospect of market penetration.

A country like Australia, whose future is indissociable from the rest of Asia, now has generous intakes of Asian immigrants. In 2009–10 (when net inward migration accounted for nearly 60 per cent of its population increase), more than half a million of its six million foreign-born inhabitants were from China or India. Australia, which has flagged up its preference for skilled migrants, is also keen to attract wealthy entrepreneurs with money to put into business or government bonds. In 2012 the immigration minister announced a new entry scheme for mega-rich investors, with an eye on China's new tycoons.

None of this is encouraging for unskilled migrants, despite the projected need for high numbers of incomers of all kinds in developed countries. That projection, of course, assumes that the overall shape of labour markets in the West will look the same in the next three decades as it did in the last two. A twenty-five-year forecast in Britain or Germany that ventured as much in the mid-1970s would have been debatable by the end of the century. By then the postwar experiment with high primary immigration into Western Europe, begun in the 1950s, was winding down: lower birth rates and higher living standards had led to a significant decline in southern European emigration, while Britain and West Germany put a stop to recruitment from further afield.

Even with zero primary migration from poorer countries, Britain and West Germany continued to receive many thousands of immigrants on grounds of family reunion, and the chain of movement set up by the first phase of recruitment survived the about-turn in host country policies. In Germany especially, returning the returnable worker became less straightforward, as foreign labour was drawn into the web of civil society. Employers' priorities often ran counter to the policy of rotation; so did the views of trade unions, solidarity organisations and immigration lawyers. When Germany ended long-term labour intakes from Turkey there were around a million Turkish residents in the country. By the early 1980s the figure was closer to 1.6 million. Many West Germans would have been happier with none at all.

The other fear in Europe as it prepared to close down primary immigration was of social division along ethnic lines: of the ghetto, segregation, the resurgence of xenophobia. In the days of the *gastarbeiter*, full citizenship in Germany was conferred by blood: blood circulates, immigrants rotate. A German was a German wherever he or she might be; a resident non-German, on the other hand, was a visitor who would in due course leave and be replaced. Or not, depending on the demand for labour. West German citizenship law was haunted by the postwar break-up of Germany and by the large numbers of Germans in the Communist East. A democratic fusion of the two was the ideal, for conservatives and liberals alike. In the interim 'relaxed coexistence' with migrants seemed to be a better answer than citizenship. But in the early years, guest workers were capsuled from the rest of society in overcrowded living quarters doing jobs that the indigenous population would not consider; the unavailability of citizenship for long-term residents and their children reinforced their otherness, while many of the rights they shared with Germans failed to protect them from hostility and outright attack. The loose-fitting garment West Germany designed for its guest workers left them vulnerable to sharp temperature falls in the host country.

Since 1999, German citizenship has become easier for foreigners to obtain, but the sense of immigration as an ambiguous experiment which, once begun, could never be done with, remains strong. Within a year of the changes in the nationality law, the General Secretary of Germany's Liberal Party called for the abolition of 'individual' right of asylum – a call, in effect, for default from the 1951 Convention – on the grounds that it was 'an invitation to abuse and to unrestricted and unregulated immigration'. The federal minister of the interior, Otto Schily, had already made a cursory division of sheep and goats a few days earlier, when he told the *Berliner Zeitung* that only 3 per cent of asylum seekers were 'genuine'. At the root of this fierce indisposition was the knowledge that asylum obligations and broader migratory pressures force governments into areas they cannot control. In 2011

Germany received 46,000 new asylum applications; it already has more than half a million refugees.

The mechanical paradigm of migration on which we still rely – 'push' in the migrant's place of origin, 'pull' in his destination – derives from the pioneering work of the geographer and statistician, Ernst Georg Ravenstein, on the results of the United Kingdom census of 1871. This model, with its two basic terms, has done sterling service for over a century. It has also undergone endless refinements by demographers. To apply to a world in which migration is on the rise, it requires two further add-ons. Both would address the odd effects that result from states attempting to regulate migration – and both are connected with the ideal of low immigration from poorer countries. The first might be thought of as 'reversal'. In its most brazen form, it is based on the belief that the way to do away with unwanted immigrants is to pour development aid into countries that produce them. The hope is that the narrative of immigration could be told differently and the socio-economic landscape quickly made over. The desired effect is a rewind of migrant influx, as large numbers of non-European males begin to retreat, heels first, towards the platform exits on the concourse of Cologne station and others totter backwards at high speed up the gangways in Marseille and Southampton.

Yet, with the right spin, 'reversal' can also be a progressive idea. It involves rethinking the economic relationship between richer and poorer countries and insisting, at the tables of the World Trade Organisation, the IMF, the World Bank and the bilateral lenders, on further, deeper debt relief, faster decartelisation of wealthy producers and more prodigal overseas aid. Advocates of liberal immigration are, in some sense, only advocates of development. Yet the real protagonist of development, they argue, is the migrant: governments must study this dedicated ferryman of aspiration and reward, and then decide how to assist him in the endless business of transfer in which he is engaged.

Immigrants have always had their own co-operative associations; often they pool their earnings: they know better than anyone the needs of the communities they have come from. 'Reversal' urges high incentives – tax relief, matching funding, low interest loans – to encourage the return of capital and skills to developing countries. Such policies, the argument runs, would enable a group of immigrants in Europe who were saving to build a school or a clinic in their place of origin to raise the money far more quickly. 'Reversal' also hopes to generate the equivalent of 'sender-country pull': it advocates import tax relief in poorer countries, the creation of foreign currency accounts with attractive interest rates and the eligibility of returnees to the same benefit entitlements, where they exist, as other nationals. In this model, the immigrant is a stakeholder in two worlds – he is 'the natural link' between North and South, and the mediating agent of a process known in France as 'co-development'.

The liberal immigration lobby, which looks on migration as a 'transitional demand' in an unfair world, believes that the more of these agents there are, the likelier the chances of achieving parity, or painless alignment, between global rich and global poor. It argues for more intensive short-term migration and more detailed matching of supply and demand, often at local levels, which would then be rubber-stamped at the national level. Crucially, enlightened 'reversal' raises the possibility of getting migrants out again, as well as letting them in – a far less dismal prospect than the moated castle of affluence, and one which distinguishes its proponents from the cruder enthusiasts of down-payment repatriation, who would happily stuff a few euros in the back pocket of an immigrant if they thought they'd seen the last of him: 10,000 French francs – worth about €4,000 in 2010 – was the sum proposed in 1977 by the administration of President Valéry Giscard d'Estaing for any Algerian who agreed to pack up and go.

Whatever the hopes invested in it, migration is a harsh process, sometimes frankly cruel, and forced migration has always involved extreme forms of triage. One has only to think of the high numbers of slave deaths in the Atlantic passage, or of the Chinese contract labour requisitioned by the New World in the latter part of the nineteenth century to compensate for the abolition of slavery. About half a million Chinese are thought to have embarked at Canton for Cuba and Peru between 1845 and 1900. Many were sold at auction when they arrived. The journey, via the Cape, took four or five months, during which 12 to 15 per cent of the passengers died. On a lesser scale, there are plentiful instances of suffering now. In November 1999, fourteen stowaways on a 12,000-tonne ferry from Greece to Italy – most of them Iraqi Kurds – were asphyxiated when a fire broke out in one of the garages. Every few months, landmines along the Greek border with Turkey kill or maim asylum seekers from Iraq. No one knows how many illegal migrants setting out on small boats from Morocco have drowned in the Strait of Gibraltar, but no one doubts a figure in the thousands.

To the clandestine migrant, however, the idea that the border may be permeable is more important than the idea that it may not be. For reluctant host states, the reverse is true. This stubborn dialectic ensures that migration remains as difficult as it always was for poorer people – and forces millions of them through an informal selection procedure, which will continue until there is no such thing as a gap in the border, an illegal migrant or a human smuggler. As another new element in the migration paradigm, it could be called 'sieving'. Its effect is, first, to separate the unfit from the fit, and then, among the fit, to recast any residual weakness as something adaptable and supple, with a high tolerance for extremes. By making it so hard for non-white contenders, the West is encouraging a rugged new species of foreign migrant. Nowhere is this more obvious than in North Africa.

Morocco 1999. A short man with a good car who knew everybody's business drove me over the border from the Spanish enclave of Ceuta. He missed the southerly road to Tetouan by a long chalk. We'd been due to make a stop there, but within an hour or two we were cruising through the outskirts of Tangier. It was a shaky start for a person who claimed to know so much. The idea was to meet a boatman, someone who ferried people across the Strait to Spain for money. There was a long wait and a brisk walk up through a busy part of the city to a teahouse where the patrons sat flicking beads in front of a European Champions' League match on the house TV. Our smuggler was charming enough – he had good-humoured, rheumy eyes and spoke passable English. The two men went back some way and, even though my guide leaned on his old acquaintance, he would not be drawn on the subject of his work. He was getting on now, and looked askance at everything about his younger days. The most he would admit to were occasional deliveries of kif and hashish to Algeciras. He struck me as a waste of time.

Even so, the old boy's name turned out to have a certain currency. A few days later, when I mentioned it in passing to another smuggler, I was rewarded with a brief glimpse into the business in Morocco. Hassan was twenty-two and came from Fez. He contracted boats to run drugs across the water; sometimes he delivered them himself. He was a laid-back, ambitious young entrepreneur with no interest in human cargo. He had met our man in Tangier and assured me he still took clandestine migrants to Spain. 'He won't say so now,' Hassan told me. 'No one will say it.' The business had fallen into disrepute – too many deaths, too much black propaganda from Europe. 'I ask you this simple question: how, under such conditions, can a man be proud of what he does?'

Hassan had no quarrel with migrant-smuggling, but it was easier and more rewarding to run drugs. Many smugglers saw it this way, he claimed, and stuck to one or the other business (the evidence for his assertion is patchy). His words came back to me many years later in Mexico, where the drugs cartels have such a strong hand in migrant smuggling. He reckoned fifteen passengers or more on a fishing smack, paying $1,300 each, couldn't match the earnings of a drugs run. In a few nights' good work a network handling drugs could recoup more than the transit value of everything the Guardia Civil confiscates in a year. With drugs, there wasn't the problem of keeping people in safe houses near the beaches for days on end and arguing down to the last dirham with every customer. If things went wrong for a migrants' agent, he couldn't heave his passengers overboard as you would a consignment of drugs. If they went badly wrong, he had other deaths to consider, along with his own, before the last prayer was offered up. 'I know your friend in Tangier,' Hassan concluded. 'And I know his business for a fact.'

Many of the illegal migrants from Morocco make their way up to the coast from poorer villages in the south. The traffickers' fees are well above average annual earnings: they represent years of family thrift and, often enough, a family debt. It is not so much the shortage of money in Morocco that impels migration – though this is acute enough for most – as the lack of schooling and medical and legal provision: access to doctors, lawyers, decent schools is prohibitively expensive for most Moroccans. But if misfortune comes between the family and their migrant – if he is repatriated, for example, or drowned – matters are very much worse than they were before they parted with their money. About 1,700 Moroccans were apprehended entering Spain illegally through Algeciras in 1997 and more than 2,000 in 1998. Each one represents a family setback in Morocco. But failure to gain entry has been the exception, for Maghrebis and sub-Saharans alike: by 2010, as the curtain came down on immigration to Spain, there were 900,000 African migrants in the country, two-thirds of whom had arrived via Morocco. Five years earlier the last in a series of amnesties for unauthorised migrants had legalised the status of at least 600,000 foreigners.

Illegal entry from the Maghreb into Spain is modest beside the flurry of human movement, most of it legal, that has begun to blur the boundaries of Mediterranean Europe and North Africa. During 1997 three million Moroccans and Europeans passed through the tiny Spanish enclave of Ceuta, tucked into the Moroccan littoral. By 1999, the figure had risen beyond five million. Millions also travel to and from Tangier. A good proportion are registered seasonal labourers in Spain's agricultural sector – an indispensable migrant workforce – while others make their way down through France in the summer, in cars and kombis loaded with goods, and back again in September for the *rentrée*. With the ferry monopoly in the Strait long gone, competitive prices and several passages daily, rates of movement are likely to increase. The waters that separate the shores of the western Maghreb and southern Spain – 14.4 kilometres at their narrowest point – now resemble what they were before the rise of nation states and machine-age empires: a transit point, rather than a barrier, between Africa and the Iberian peninsula.

Many sub-Saharan migrants head for the Mediterranean. Some hope to claim asylum in Europe, but the great majority are looking for a livelihood. Most travel north along the arduous routes from West Africa – so far, no more than a few thousand every year – but here, the phenomenon of migration from poor countries is at its most simple and stark. Poverty, frustration and danger are the main motives for leaving. It nonetheless takes willpower and a particular cast of character to make the journey.

Year after year, African commentators, World Bank officials, foreign news editors and aid agencies wet a finger and raise it in the hope of detecting a new wind of change on the continent. There are always signs of improvement; it's a matter of looking for them. The *Economist* reports that between 2011 and 2015 seven of the world's ten fastest-growing economies will be sub-Saharan. In 2010 there were around 2.2 million refugees in the region, a steep fall since the mid-1990s. Yet conflict and deprivation remain the handmaidens of post-colonial politics in much of the continent. It is a common misconception that the very few illegal migrants who make it out of sub-Saharan Africa are no better off than those who stay. Smugglers' fees and other costs can run into thousands of dollars, which proves the existence of money somewhere in the family of a typical 'illegal' heading for the rich world. The destitute too can still get to Europe, on loans, charity or ingenuity. Both the poor and the not so poor have made the calculation that matters may only get worse if they remain where they are. A young father knows that, if he does not die before his time, he may well outlive his own children; another sees the painstaking work of generations withering in a dustbowl of mismanagement and corruption. Whether it is a threat or already a reality, ruin is what hounds the sub-Saharan migrant up through the desert.

For West Africans heading north in the 1990s, there was a 'left side' and a 'right side'. The fulcrum was somewhere in Niger. The easterly route took them up through Libya. The itineraries and transactions were obscure. Turkish smugglers might ferry migrants to a large boat at anchor off Izmir, slowly filling up with other clients – typically Kurds – and then head west into European waters to decant them into smaller vessels. This, perhaps, was the way that the men from Sierra Leone had come – a fantastically roundabout way – before I saw them brought off the old hulk in Santa Maria di Leuca in Italy.

The 'left side', or westerly route, involves a journey through Algeria, Morocco and often the two Spanish seaboard enclaves of Ceuta and Melilla, remnants of Spain's imperial holdings in Africa. The demise of this modest empire, at the time of Franco's death, led to the creation of what is now one of the oldest refugee encampments in the world, as the inhabitants of Spanish Sahara fled Moroccan annexation and settled in Algeria. About 250,000 Saharans are still waiting in the Algerian camps for an opportunity to return. Spain has managed to parry Moroccan designs on Ceuta and Melilla, however, and so, on its entry into the European Community in 1986, two forward posts of the future Union came into existence on the continent of Africa.

Ceuta is no more than twenty square kilometres, with a population of 75,000. It is modern, artificially and lavishly developed in places by mainland subsidies, and unmistakably a garrison community with a visible military presence. As EU territory in Africa, it is another of Europe's frontline defences against migrant intrusion. It also provides for those whom it has failed to intercept at the Moroccan border, settling them in a large camp and eventually processing them onto the mainland. I made three visits to the camp at the end of 1998, when there were fewer than a thousand inmates, but it had, they said, been much fuller. It was set off the coast road at a place called Calamocarro.

You passed a row of fishing boats drawn up on the beaches and, a little way on, you could see a public phone box with a queue of Africans. You walked up over a steep gravel terrace to find dozens of Spanish Army tents pitched in a grove of eucalyptus. By day, the camp had the generous, all-comer smell of the open markets in parts of southern Africa: sweet soap; weatherproof plastics trounced by rain; fritters; okra, oil and chili. The wind gusting off the sea brought the sharp, medicated scent of eucalyptus beyond the confines of the settlement.

One section of the camp consisted of a small Algerian detachment – a handful of tents containing perhaps twenty families, most of them fleeing the violence of a long civil conflict. In one tent a young couple and their three children had been installed for ten weeks, waiting for news of an asylum application. The mother was an educated twenty-one-year-old from Oran who had been working before they left. Her father had been murdered by an Islamist faction the previous year; later she, too, had been threatened. Her husband was a security guard for the state petroleum company; as a government employee, he was also a target. They'd been relieved of their savings by the Moroccan frontier police and were now defenceless. It would not have done to send them back through Morocco to the butcher's war over the border.

The tension between the Algerians and sub-Saharans was unmistakable. Many sub-Saharans felt strongly that there should be some form of 'economic asylum' on the grounds that the atrophy of their economies had gone hand in hand with the erosion of human and political rights. They looked with a sidelong, dubious glance at the asylum seeker's bitter privilege. Others spoke well of the kindness they'd been shown while travelling through Algeria.

One morning in the camp, a giant of a man from Cameroon called Joseph announced that Algeria might be a dangerous place for Algerians, but 'not for us blacks'. He couldn't say why – 'Perhaps it's something in the Qur'an.' Joseph was twenty-five. He had crossed most of the Sahara on foot and could tell you the time it had taken him, from the day he left home to the day he reached Ceuta, with the precision of a man who had chalked up each sunrise on the floor of a vast, shimmering cell whose walls were an infinite distance from any point at which he woke. The total, which he was apt to repeat, came to 181 days. Joseph had nearly died of dehydration, but had been saved by nomads, who looked after him for a week or more and sent him on his way with a sack of powdered sugar and a skin of water. He insisted, in defence of the Algerians, that no one could know whether their asylum applications would be approved. He refused to join in a whispering campaign against them. Like several fellow Cameroonians, he was intent on mainland Europe. 'I'll do anything provided it's legal.' Though he had been driven north by poverty, he wanted to campaign for radical change in his country, just as any political exile might. Economic misery can make a dissident of almost anyone.

Joseph fraternised with the Algerians, towering over them like an illustrious tree, whose shade they invariably sought. He was on hand to argue their rights when it came to mealtimes – Spanish military rations delivered twice daily – or hustling for extra blankets, or barter disputes over fritters and cigarettes. He also tended recent arrivals from West Africa. He took a man about ten years older than himself under his care as soon as he appeared in the camp: a courteous wraith in a green woollen hat emblazoned with a 'Red Raiders' logo. His complexion was sallow after four months on the road and a long stint in the desert. 'You must be strong-backed to do this thing, especially going through Morocco,' he remarked while he waited for Joseph to negotiate a double helping of meat for him at the head of the food queue. 'They will take everything from you and beat you, I mean beat you so hard.' Moments later, his teeth began chattering and he gasped out a verdict on the journey he had made: 'No. Definitely I would not accept that my worst enemy should come this way.' He started laughing, then shaking, wrenching the hat from his head and coughing into it until I thought he would die, but when Joseph handed him a mountainous plate of food, he set about it with conviction.

Something open-hearted and alert about these people who had crossed the desert gave them the edge over the Algerians, who kept to their tents when they could, musing darkly over the bloodshed in which they'd been caught up, like so many of their forebears. Old racial stereotypes, almost obsolete now, were being revived by circumstance at this unlikely point of entry into Europe: the valiant African, the resentful Arab, the severe but tolerant white man, presiding over the destiny of the lesser races.

Calamocarro was an ill-lit place at night, full of milling, hooded shadows in anoraks. The ground was muddy, the air dank and the temperature too low for anyone's comfort. There were seldom more than two soldiers to oversee the throng of migrants. Apart from the odd scuffle, the camp was self-regulating, but in the darkness, it felt sombre and a little edgy. It was after dark, however, that people spoke freely and it would have been around seven or eight o'clock on a bitter night that Williams Osunde loomed out from the tent placements and introduced himself. Williams was twenty. He had come from Lagos, where he threw over his studies when his father, then his extended family, were unable to support him. He drifted around for a time until it struck him that whichever way the cards fell, he had no future in Nigeria. One may as well come to an early end as waste away, so why not attempt the journey to Europe? 'Even we prefer dying here to dying there,' he said of the decision to leave. 'By now I was a realist, you see.'

Williams Osunde set out in a party of six, each of whom paid about £50 for a place on a 'camion' north to Sokoto. Here they paid another trucker to take them across the border and into Niger. Immigration at Niger relieved them of a further £50 per person. They hung about scraping funds together in Niger, working as water-carriers and shoeshine boys, and meeting more young people from other parts of Nigeria, Ghana and Cameroon who were on the same trail. After two months in Niger they set off north on foot, fifteen people by now. A six-day march brought them within striking distance of the Algerian border. They pooled their resources to engage the services of a smuggler, who took the money, put them in a truck but dropped them well short of the frontier. They walked the remaining eighty kilometres.

At the frontier, they waited several days for an opportune moment to cross. Here, one of their party died of thirst. Williams no longer recalled the stages or the place names on the next leg of the journey. It seems that they continued on the road running north from Niger, pressed on through Algeria to In Salah and cut west to join another north-south road leading up to the Moroccan border – a journey of about 1,800 kilometres, some of it by truck, but most of it on foot. So far as they knew, and they were delirious for long periods, they crossed the Algerian Sahara in two months, the truck rides enabling them to strike an average of thirty kilometres a day. By the time they entered Morocco, four more of their party had died.

Williams was about to describe what became of him in Morocco, when an eerie voice some way behind him in the darkness began chanting: 'Row, row, row your boat, gently down the stream.' It broke off abruptly and a broad figure in a parka, face indistinguishable, was striding through the shadows towards us with one arm raised, as if in anger.

'Tell him, Williams,' said the voice in the depths of the parka, 'how our country produces 2.1 million barrels of oil a day and how we are starving. Nigeria, Federal Republic of Embezzlers.'

The young man in the parka had been one of Williams's party and now he urged him to divulge more about the journey. When Williams could not, or would not, it was his companion who explained how they had eaten leaves, sucked up the water from pools of sandy mud and drunk their own urine; how one of them was stabbed through the ribs during an argument with strangers and another had died of snakebite. He spoke of 'trekking' to the point of death, of seeming to die on his feet, falling into an abyss of exhaustion, only to be resurrected in the furnace of the late morning.

'Africans are strong,' said Williams. 'God just make them so.'

'Merrily, merrily, merrily, merrily ...' the dark mouth in the shadow of the parka intoned, and again: 'Two point one million, my friend, two *point* one.'

At the Moroccan border, Williams and the remaining survivors were taken into custody by the police. Only one escaped.

'Upon all your suffering,' Williams concluded, 'upon all your trekking, upon all your danger, they will put you back.'

Like several people from other parties who had reached Calamocarro, they were then dumped by the Moroccans back on the border with Algeria – 'Algeria's that way' – crossed it by stealth and re-entered Morocco later by another route, several days' hike further north. Everyone in the camp who was prepared to talk complained of ill-treatment in Morocco, and of being robbed of their last throw – a tradable watch, a low-carat gem, a nugget of gold – by the police. They claimed to have been beaten. And the three or four women – who had been brought along precisely because they were negotiating-counters in the event of an impasse – had been raped.

The last leg of the journey through Morocco to Ceuta brings those who have survived the Algerian desert and Moroccan hospitality to a low range of hills. Here they must wait, perhaps for several days, studying the Spanish military and police patrols around the border perimeter between the enclave and Morocco. Once there is a gap in the patrol schedule or propitious weather – low cloud, mist on the hills – they will make their bid for European territory. If they cross successfully and elude the chase, the great majority will be allowed to remain. Anyone caught on or near the perimeter is put back inside Morocco. Those are the rules. Success is a matter of luck and, eventually, persistence: nobody who has come this far will give up after one failure. In 1997, about 700 illegal migrants entered Ceuta this way. The tally for the following year was nearer 1,000. For 1999, it was 7,000. A year-on-year increase projected on these figures alone looked intriguing. Most of the people who got across came overland; about 40 per cent – wealthier, one must assume – flew to Casablanca and made their way to the hills overlooking the perimeter with the help of Moroccan guides.

The EU knows that Ceuta and Melilla are vulnerable flanks of Fortress Europe, and that migrant pressure has to be opposed at these tempting points of transgression. In 1993 it approved funding for a defensive wall around Ceuta, running for eight kilometres and consisting of two parallel wire fences, 2.5 metres high and five metres apart. Between the wire fences a line of sensors was installed; lamps were set every thirty-three metres and thirty closed circuit cameras were spaced along the perimeter. Rolls of razor wire were laid beneath the nearside fence. Eighty-four culverts in the low ground where the border runs were cemented in. Round-the-clock patrols went into operation. The cost has been estimated at $25 million. Yet the long wire barrier stretching over the brown hills is no more than a term in the same game that sets clandestine migrants against wealthy countries further north: a line that must be reached and crossed, just as the trembling path of moonlight and the wake of the Italian patrol boats in the Otranto Channel are lines of jeopardy to be avoided. In both places the poor pit their wits against the technological expertise of the rich.

Alfonso Cruzado, the stocky, bespectacled officer of the Guardia Civil (the Spanish gendarmerie) who showed me round the perimeter, suggested I scale one of the wire walls in the double defence. It took about forty-five seconds. Balancing for the turn at the top, where the only handhold is a straight line of clipped wire, I cut both hands. Cruzado said he had watched migrants take both fences in less than twenty seconds and wade through the razor wire, slashing their legs to shreds. If you have a bull at your back, he observed, you're ready to run for your life. Like many of the British military involved in the withdrawal from Palestine, Cruzado and his colleagues were troubled by the fate to which they had abandoned their largest North African possession, the Spanish Sahara, in a botched decolonisation process that sent most of the inhabitants into indefinite exile as refugees in Algeria. They saw the whole continent in the light of that failure and found it hard to put the burden of blame for its misfortunes on Africans.

'What colonial power seriously tried to develop an infrastructure in its African possessions?' Captain José Rebollo, one of Cruzado's superiors, asked when I suggested that the migrants who made it over the perimeter were very far from being down-trodden or defeated. The best answer to this question would surely have been: 'Not the Spanish or the Portuguese.' But Rebollo added quickly that it was a mistake to attribute the force which drove migrants to their own strength of character, when it was so evidently a material issue of misery – and history.

'What power ever attempted to play down tribal differences?' he went on. 'And when Africa was distributed to the Europeans, was the division not done with a ruler? We, the colonial powers, are reaping what we sowed. The sub-Saharans who get here are people fleeing death and hunger.'

No one I met in the Guardia Civil appeared to disagree with this, and none believed the perimeter would be a match for such powerful motives or for such an intractable past. One or two said that if they'd been born into a world of hardship and bad govern-ance, as many sub-Saharans are, they would take the same course. They had a measured disdain for Moroccan illegals, who thanks to a repatriation accord they would turf back over the frontier, even if they were found inside the city. The Moroccans must face the perils of the Strait if they want to reach the EU, or try to hide in trucks on the ferries: hundreds of young stowaways are caught and returned every year. The Guardia Civil were not keen, either, on wealthier sub-Saharans, chiefly from francophone countries, who they claimed to have found in Calamocarro with mobile phones (rarer in the 1990s than they are now) and thousands of dollars. On the rest, however, they looked sympathetically, even conscientiously. So did the civilian administration in Ceuta. The Spanish authorities undertake to 'regularise' migrants who reach the enclave and, if possible, to find them jobs. There are weekly work details and, in due course, as the paperwork on each migrant is completed, a one-year renewable work permit allows them onto the Spanish mainland.

As for the perimeter, neither civilian nor military personnel thought of it as a barrier. The expensive high-tech edifice at the margins of Fortress Europe was a filter only, which might thin down the numbers of uninvited to about 300 a year. This was a target figure from the governor's office, yet the spokesman who supplied it was doubtful. 'Directly beneath us,' he said, 'is a continent in crisis. It's not yet alarming, but it's going to grow, slowly, incrementally, and we must prepare for something very much larger.' He was working on the assumption that by 2014 anything between fifteen and twenty million migrants would have made a bid for entry into Western Europe via Spain.

Rebollo, an old military man with a soldier's interest in history, saw things in much the same way. Migration had usually been from poor parts of the world to richer ones – 'What was it that drove the Barbarians to Rome?' he asked – but he was persuaded that migrations from the North lacked the staying power of those from the South. It was a very Spanish perspective, which he brought up to date by citing the per capita GDP of Morocco ($1,200 at the time) relative to that of Spain ($15,000) – a modest difference, as it happens, beside the comparative purchasing power of an Austrian citizen (75.7 in PPP), against that of a Nigerian (3.0) or a Sierra Leonean (1.4). Rebollo felt that something had to give. To predict how it would happen, he had turned the push-pull model of migration into an atmospheric chart and now forecast an incoming hurricane whose early warning was a spate of dust-devils wriggling north across the scrublands of the Sahel.

In 1999, the perimeter around Ceuta was once more deemed inadequate against the low technologies of willpower and mutiny. The authorities decided to increase the surveillance capacity along its length – more cameras, better sensors – in the hope that the numbers who get across will dwindle to a level that the EU finds acceptable. Increasingly, sub-Saharan migrants, like many Moroccans, have been forced to contemplate the frightening option of the Strait, divert to the Canary Islands – another dangerous stretch of water – or work their way up the 'right side' of the continent, forging a more dependable chain of contacts as they head for the smuggling markets of Libya and Turkey.

Europe, meanwhile, has devised a very fine form of 'sieving' for illegal migrants from Africa: by reaching the safety of the camp, the able and resourceful define the quality of the intake. They, in turn, are drawn from a larger contingent who self-selected earlier on by leaving their countries of origin and submitting to the trans-Saharan ordeal. Many survivors of the Sahara, moreover, have already distinguished themselves from millions of in-country migrants who abandon the harsh conditions of rural Africa for those of Lagos, Accra, Abidjan, Kinshasa, Bamako, Yaoundé, Dakar. Whether the favoured few end up picking fruit in Almería, cleaning the toilets in the Bibliothèque Nationale, working for an NGO in Geneva, running a vice racket in Milan or an African Studies module in Leiden, these job-seekers are among the most highly motivated in Europe.

There is something puzzling about sub-Saharan Africa's place in the pattern of intercontinental migration. The anecdotal evidence of those Africans who have made it to Europe reinforces the model of desperation as the great push – stronger than any more sophisticated ambition, fired by the rise of a regional economy. Yet, if it is true that things in Africa can get no worse – as optimists concluded in the mid-1990s – then in due course the numbers of migrants will increase all the same. Rebollo and his men will have been right for the wrong reasons. War, hunger and social breakdown may not have caused massive numbers of people to migrate north beyond the natural boundary of the Sahara, but the first glimmerings of prosperity may well inspire higher numbers of Africans to come to Europe.

What, though, if Rebollo were right for the reasons he gave? It is possible, after all, that globalisation will continue to blur the recent picture of international migration, in which abject poverty does not produce the same degree of migratory pressure from developing countries as relative wealth. The ambiguities, at that point, might merely multiply, as climate change adds to the array of reasons for humans to move across borders, so that migrants from the poorest economies begin to press towards rich states with more insistence, alongside others who have already taken their cue from an increase in living standards.

It's hard in any case to deny the long-standing truth about human movement, stirring beneath the huge weight of scholarly work on migration, that desperation is a powerful engine of resolve. It's a truth we begin to grasp when, at the end of an unimaginable journey, a young woman from West Africa in the seventh month of her pregnancy scales two high fences, fights her way through a roll of razor wire and enters Europe by a little Spanish garrison in the Maghreb. This petitioner at the rich man's gate was one of a dozen or more who crossed into Ceuta while I was going in and out of the camp at Calamocarro. She was caught on the perimeter road and it looked very much as if she knew the rules of the game: the Guardia Civil had planned to make an exception in her case – or so they said – but when they put her in a cell overnight before transferring her to the camp, she committed suicide. Nobody established her country of origin or even her real name.

For a day or two her death was all over the Spanish press. It also stirred up a passionate sense of solidarity in Calamocarro. Williams Osunde was so distressed by the news that he insisted on attending the funeral, though he had never met her. At the graveside he read from Ephesians: 'For we wrestle not against the flesh and blood, but against principalities, against powers, against the rulers of the darkness of this world, against spiritual wickedness in high places.' The way Williams saw it, there were two domains, that of the rich and that of the poor; and there was a scandalous conspiracy to ensure that those from the second who needed to reach the first were prevented from doing so.

Injustice is the moral force in this account and it is undeniable. Yet necessity plays the greater role in the story of human movement, referring us back to older, more local migrations in Africa and other parts of the world, where mobility was bound up with the search for pasture and livelihood. When you stand at the outer limits of Europe and gaze into Morocco, confident that at any moment there are at least four or five people concealed in the folds of the hills or lying low in tiny huts, watching the Spanish border patrols and weighing up their moment, the idea of necessity is impossible to set aside. Day after day, year after year, the members of the Guardia Civil in Ceuta and Melilla scrutinise the terrain on the other side of their frontiers. No argument is likely to shake their belief in the idea that it is lack and fear that drive people north to trespass on the rich grasslands of mainland Europe.

A built facility has since replaced the woodland camp at Calamocarro, and the numbers entering Spanish North Africa are far fewer than public officials in Ceuta had predicted. Around Melilla, the other Spanish enclave on the coast of Morocco, the barrier was reinforced in 2005. Five to six thousand unauthorised migrants entered Ceuta and Melilla in that year, several hundred during a co-ordinated assault on both enclaves when migrants charged the fences. In Ceuta, Moroccan security opened fire from the rear while the Guardia pelted the assailants with rubber bullets. There were more than a dozen deaths and fifty injuries. But the fears haunting the governor's office in Ceuta in the 1990s that millions of migrants would stream through the defences have proved unfounded. In 2010 fewer than 1,600 people breached Spain's North African enclaves.

Calamitous predictions, such as the UN Environmental Programme's suggestion in 2005 that there might by 2010 be fifty million climate refugees, are the hyperbole of immigration and asylum arguments. Then again, more reliable figures, like the Spanish government's record for unlawful entries, tell a part of the story only: the missing element here is that many migrants who would have tried to enter via Spain are now moving up through different routes that take them into Greece. Migrants will go where necessity impels them to go and this will give rise to injustices – flight, refoulement, a pointless suicide in custody. Where human movement across borders is concerned, the culture of rights and the reality of needs are still a good way apart.

In the epic of Sundiata, the thirteenth-century warrior-king who founds the ancient empire of Mali, the hero begins life as a cripple. The blacksmiths forge crutches for him, but they buckle when he tries to use them. On the day before his circumcision, however,

Sundiata raises his arms, grips the eaves of his mother's house and pulls himself upright. He reaches out to a baobab tree, tears it from the ground and sets it down at the doorway of the house. In this dramatic transition from broken child to emperor, the extent of an earlier debility is now the measure of a new-found strength. Like Sundiata, the champions who manage to reach Europe by luck and endurance have wrung strength from weakness, but they have had to draw on the kinds of fundamental resources that are not replenished automatically. Whatever else they are, they remain fugitives, like anyone trying to escape the clutches of a dictatorship or a party of religious zealots. In the past, refugees have won greater international sympathy than economic migrants. Theirs has been the more identifiable grievance: at its source there is often an identifiable persecutor. Yet the order of economic difficulty that prevails in some parts of the world is akin to persecution. No consensus exists about the identity of the tormentor, and so those who try to put it behind them are more easily reviled than others fleeing the attentions of secret police or state militias.

Once again, little solace here for the economic migrant from a poor country, even though the resolve of impoverished people to breach the walls of the wealthy economies has a political character, for it involves defiance as well as despair. It is not their political opinion so much as their political predicament that puts them in danger. Their first enemy is grinding attrition in their own country; their second, no less formidable, is to be found in the countries on which they have set their hearts, where governments still move with a pitiful sloth towards debt cancellation and fair trade, and where the illegal migrant is regarded as a cutpurse. Most people who migrate away from misery are politicised; they have the facts and figures somewhere at the back of their minds. A man like Joseph who set out from Cameroon in 1998 to look for a job in Europe would have known that his country's debt stood at nine billion dollars, and that every year the sum of interest and principal due for repayment was higher than national export earnings. He would have despised his government as a coterie of irresponsible villains. He would have seen many lives turn to dust.

He would also have understood that none of this could amount to mitigation, in the eyes of the rich world, once he forced his way in. Realising in the end that he was on his own, he would have struck out anyhow.

Notes and Acknowledgments

Many more of the sources on which the earlier edition of this book drew are now on the Internet. I've omitted original references to statistical material that's since been superseded or can be accessed on the websites of any UN agency, including UNHCR, and other bodies such as the International Organisation for Migration and the OECD. Where they are still cited, it is because they are not available to download (e.g. *Trends in International Migration*, SOPEMI/OECD, 1998).

Regular publications by UNHCR and the IOM including *The State of the World's Refugees* (annual) and *World Migration Report* (annual) are among the most useful statistical sources on asylum and migration worldwide in the last twenty years. So are publications by the OECD's Continuous Reporting System on Migration (SOPEMI).

For analytical sources on migration, I've relied on briefings and articles published online by the Global Detention Project in Geneva; the Migration Policy Institute, the Pew Research Center and the Pew Hispanic Center in Washington; the Institute for Public Policy Research and Migrants' Rights Network in London; the Centre on Policy, Migration and Society (COMPAS) and the International Migration Institute in Oxford; and the regional websites of the Panos Institute.

For the epigraphs: Claude Lévi-Strauss, *Tristes Tropiques*, translated by John and Doreen Weightman (Atheneum, 1974), Eric Ambler, *The Mask of Demetrios* (Hodder & Stoughton, 1939), Sembène Ousmane, *'The Money Order' with 'White Genesis': Two*

Novellas, translated by Clive Wake (Heinemann, 1972), Richard Rodriguez, *Days of Obligation: An Argument with my Mexican Father* (Viking Penguin, 1992), Ghassan Kanafani, *'Men in the Sun' and Other Palestinian Stories*, translated by Hilary Kilpatrick (Rienner, 1999).

The names of several informants in Italy, the UK, Mexico and the US have been changed.

Europe 1998–2000: Chapters 1, 2 and 5

For numbers arriving illegally on the coast of Italy, 1998–99, the Guardia di Finanza offices in Otranto and the *Economist*, 16 October 1999.

For women trafficked into the EU, Phil Williams (ed.), *Illegal Immigration and Commercial Sex: The New Slave Trade* (Frank Cass, 1999), especially G. J. N. Bruinsma and G. Meershoek, 'Organised Crime and Trafficking in Women from Eastern Europe in the Netherlands'.

For forced movement in Europe from the late nineteenth century until the early 1950s, John Hope Simpson (ed.), *The Refugee Problem: Report of a Survey* (Oxford, 1939); Tony Kushner and Katharine Knox, *Refugees in an Age of Genocide* (Frank Cass, 1999) and Hannah Arendt, *The Origins of Totalitarianism* (Harcourt Brace Jovanovitch, 1951).

For percentages of Zaireans (nowadays DRC Congolese), Sri Lankans and Somalis with refugee status in Canada and the UK during the 1990s, and research staff available to adjudicators in the UK and Australia, *Providing Protection: Towards Fair and Effective Asylum Procedures* (Justice/Immigration Law Practitioners' Association/Asylum Rights Campaign, 1997).

For Bosnian asylum seekers in Germany, asylum application totals in Germany in 1992 and deaths of clandestine migrants, *Migration News Sheet*, now available online.

For numbers of Africans, West Indians and Asians entering the UK from the late 1950s onwards, Ian Spencer, *British Immigration Policy since 1939* (Routledge, 1997).

For digests of the Human Development Index and PPP tables, the annual *Pocket World in Figures* (Profile/*Economist*).

For predicted shortages of under-sixty-fives in rich countries at the end of the twentieth century, SOPEMI's *Trends in International Migration* of 1998 (OECD).

For Chinese migrant labour to the Americas, Gérard Chaliand and Jean-Pierre Rageau, *The Penguin Atlas of Diasporas* (Viking Penguin, 1995).

For Somali smugglers, Nuruddin Farah, *Yesterday, Tomorrow: Voices from the Somali Diaspora* (Cassell, 2000).

For the Cold War and the 1951 Convention Relating to the Status of Refugees, Danièle Joly, 'A New Asylum Regime in Europe', in Frances Nicholson and Patrick Twomey (eds), *Refugee Rights and Realities: Evolving International Concepts and Regimes* (Cambridge, 1998).

For the story of the *Cheshire*, the evacuation of Belgians to Britain in 1914, the anti-Belgian riots and the revolt of the Basque children in Kent, Kushner and Knox, 1999.

For the British press and asylum seekers, *Daily Mail*, 3 February 1900 (quoted in Kushner and Knox) and 6 October 1998, *News of the World*, 26 July 2009 and *Jewish Chronicle*, 4 June 1999.

For the rise of the 'colour bar' in the UK, Spencer, 1997.

For the Ugandan trader turned asylum seeker, Hirit Belai, *London Review of Books*, 18 July 1996.

For the 'Kosovan' African in Calais, *Libération*, 22 August 1999.

W. H. Auden's poem can be found in the revised *Collected Poems* (Faber, 2007).

For the Amsterdam Treaty, Ben Hall and Ashish Bhatt, *Policing Europe: EU Justice and Home Affairs Co-operation* (London, Centre for European Reform, 1999).

The 'draft action plans' of the High Level Working Group were discussed at a special meeting of the European Council in Tampere, Finland, 15 and 16 October 1999.

For background on indigenous Italian migration, John Foot, 'Immigration and the City: Milan and Mass Immigration, 1958–98' in *Modern Italy*, 4 (2), 1999.

John Berger and Jean Mohr, *A Seventh Man* (1975) was republished by Verso in 2010.

Susan George, *The Lugano Report: On Preserving Capitalism in the 21st Century* was published in a new edition by Pluto in 2003.

For the shortcomings of the 1951 Convention Relating to the Status of Refugees and the 1967 Protocol, 'The Refugee Convention: Why not scrap it?', a Chatham House discussion with Guy Godwin-Gill, 20 October 2005.

For climate change migration, the Environmental Justice Foundation, in particular Rizwana Hasan, 'Climate Change and Migration: Forced Displacement, "Climate Refugees" and the Need for a New Legal Instrument' (EJF briefing paper, 2011).

For Yaguine Koita and Fodé Tounkara, Alex Duval-Smith, 'The boys who froze to death at 40,000 feet', *Independent*, 1 September 1999.

E. G. Ravenstein's analysis of the 1871 census of the British Isles was reprinted from the *Geographical Magazine* as *The Birthplace of the People and the Laws of Migration* by Trübner (1876).

For updated figures on numbers of people being trafficked worldwide and the global value of the business, *Trafficking in Persons Report 2010* (US State Department, online).

Europe 2012: Chapter 3

Recent statistical material in Chapter 3 on Britain and the rest of the European Union is drawn extensively from Eurostat, Frontex and the Global Detention Project.

Baukje Prinz, 'The Nerve to Break Taboos' appeared in the *Journal of International Migration and Integration*, 3 (3 & 4), 2002.

Thilo Sarrazin, *Deutschland schafft sich ab: Wie wir unser Land aufs Spiel setzen* is published by Deutsche Verlags-Anstalt, 2010.

For arguments in Britain about migrants and the public purse, Carlos Vargas-Silva's briefing paper 'The Fiscal Impact of Immigration in the UK' (Migration Observatory, 2011) and Dhananjayan Sriskandarajah, Laurence Cooley and Howard

Reed, *Paying their Way: The Fiscal Contribution of Migrants in the UK* (IPPR, 2005). IPPR has also addressed the subject of unauthorised migration (Tim Finch and Miriam Cherti, *No Easy Options: Irregular Immigration in the UK*, 2011).

For UK government pledges on immigration targets, Alan Travis, 'Cameron's empty immigration promise', *Guardian*, 11 January 2010.

A new translation of Frantz Fanon's *Black Skin, White Masks* (1952) by Richard Philcox is published by Grove Press, 2008.

For UK deportation costs per capita, *Final Report: Costing Work Stream – NAO Asylum Study* (Accenture, 2008).

For Tariq Modood on Muslim identity, 'Muslims and the Politics of Difference' in Sarah Spencer (ed.), *The Politics of Migration: Managing Opportunity, Conflict and Change* (*Political Quarterly* special issue, 2003).

For negative effects of migrants on healthcare, education, housing and UK fiscality, all briefings by Migration Watch UK.

For Paul Scheffer on institutional rites of passage for migrants in Europe, *Immigrant Nations* (Polity, 2011).

For the richest 2 per cent of adults owning half the world's wealth, 'The World Distribution of Household Wealth' (World Institute for Development Economics Research of the United Nations University [UNU-WIDER], 2006).

For Gadaffi's migration co-operation agenda, 'Libya Detention Profile', Global Detention Project (2009) and *Boundary News* (International Boundaries Research Unit, Durham, April 2012).

For shifting routes to Europe from sub-Saharan Africa, Hein de Haas, 'Trans-Saharan Migration to North Africa and the EU', Migration Policy Institute (November 2006) and 'Europe Fighting Irregular Migration – Consequences for West African Mobility', Danish Institute for International Studies (October 2011).

George Kennan's memo of 1948 can be read in full at Wikisource.

For the morality of borders, Christopher Heath Wellman and Phillip Cole, *Debating the Ethics of Immigration: Is There a Right to Exclude?* (Oxford, 2011).

For Régis Debray on borders, *Eloge des frontières* (Gallimard, 2010).

For detention in Mauritania, *European Borders: Controls, Detentions and Deportations, 2009/10*, Migreurop annual report, 2010.

For arrests at the border between Turkey and Greece, *Voice of America* News, 14 March 2011.

For gang activity along the Channel coast, 'Quand les migrants disent stop au racket des passeurs', Association Terre d'errance, terreerrance.wordpress.com, 26 September 2009.

For camp-breaking in Igoumenitsa, *Clandestina: Migration and Struggle in Greece*, clandestinenglish.wordpress.com

The Americas 2012: Chapter 4

Much statistical material on Arizona and Mexico is drawn from the Pew Research Center and the Pew Hispanic Center, including Hispanic population totals, school numbers, jobless numbers, as well as estimates for unauthorised and authorised residents by state and in the US as a whole.

The Humane Borders 'deaths map' can be found at humaneborders.org.

See also Margaret Regan, *The Death of Josseline: Immigration Stories from the Arizona/Mexico Borderlands* (Beacon, 2010) and Luis Alberto Urrea, *The Devil's Highway* (Little, Brown, 2004).

For Pima County crime figures, '2010 Statistics', County Sheriff's Department, pimasheriff.org.

For incarceration in Arizona, Daryl R. Fischer, *Prisoners in Arizona: A Profile of the Inmate Population* (Arizona Prosecuting Attorneys' Advisory Council, 2010), Jonathan Clark, 'Federal inmates start filling beds at new county jail', *Nogales International*, 26 May 2011 and Tom Barry, *Border Wars* (MIT, 2011).

For drugs seizures on and around the border, 'Feds attribute surging seizure stats to more manpower, technology', *Homeland Security Newswire*, 8 December 2010.

For numbers of Hispanics leaving Arizona or losing jobs, Magnus Lofstrom, Sarah Bohn and Steven Raphael, 'Lessons from the 2007 Legal Arizona Workers Act', Public Policy Institute of California, 2011.

For William Finnegan on Sheriff Arpaio, 'Sheriff Joe', *New Yorker*, 20 July 2009.

For NPR's investigation of ALEC, Russell Pearce and the boom in private prison facilities, Laura Sullivan, 'Prison economics help drive Arizona immigration law', *NPR*, 28 October 2010.

For a breakdown of the deportations under Obama's presidency, Adam Serwer, 'Obama getting close to one million deportations', *Mother Jones*, 9 September 2011.

For Partnership for a New American Economy's position on immigration, renewoureconomy.org.

For unemployment in Ciudad Juárez, Emily Schmall, *Daily Finance*, 20 April 2010.

2666 by Roberto Bolaño is translated by Natasha Wimmer and published by Picador, 2006.

For US Border Patrol estimates of one apprehension for every three crossings on the US/Mexico border, 'Judicial Watch obtains new Border Patrol apprehension statistics for illegal alien smugglers and "special interest aliens"', *Judicial Watch* press room, 9 March 2011.

There are many people to thank for this book. Don Flynn read and discussed the original manuscript while he was at the Joint Council for the Welfare of Immigrants in London in the 1990s. In 2011, as the director of Migrants' Rights Network, he took up from where we'd left off. Jan Brulc, also at MRN, went over the later European chapter with an eagle eye for figures and trends. Laurie Fransman at Garden Court Chambers read the original manuscript in its entirety and offered invaluable legal advice. Margaret Regan and Kevin Gosner did the same for the chapter on Arizona and Mexico. I'm indebted for help and intelligence on the ground, in various countries, to Lorna Scott Fox, Valentina Agostinis, Alfredo Gutiérrez, Sharon Zapata, Andrew Hsiao,

Mathieu Quinette, Miranda Spieler, Isabel García and Jeta Xharra. The *London Review of Books* funded the earlier research and published the results in 1999. The later chapters also appeared in the *LRB* in 2011 and 2012: my thanks to all my colleagues at the paper. I'm especially grateful to Tariq Ali and Jacob Stevens for suggesting an updated version, to Lorna Scott Fox for assembling the parts as a whole and to Verso for enabling me to get to Arizona and Mexico.